ROUTLEDGE LIBRARY EDITIONS: EDUCATION AND RELIGION

Volume 2

RELIGIOUS EDUCATION 5–12

RELIGIOUS EDUCATION 5–12

DEREK BASTIDE

Taylor & Francis Group
LONDON AND NEW YORK

First published in 1987 by The Falmer Press

This edition first published in 2019
by Routledge
2 Park Square, Milton Park, Abingdon, Oxon OX14 4RN

and by Routledge
52 Vanderbilt Avenue, New York, NY 10017

Routledge is an imprint of the Taylor & Francis Group, an informa business

© 1987 D. Bastide

All rights reserved. No part of this book may be reprinted or reproduced or utilised in any form or by any electronic, mechanical, or other means, now known or hereafter invented, including photocopying and recording, or in any information storage or retrieval system, without permission in writing from the publishers.

Trademark notice: Product or corporate names may be trademarks or registered trademarks, and are used only for identification and explanation without intent to infringe.

British Library Cataloguing in Publication Data
A catalogue record for this book is available from the British Library

ISBN: 978-0-367-13819-6 (Set)
ISBN: 978-0-429-05630-7 (Set) (ebk)
ISBN: 978-0-367-14207-0 (Volume 2) (hbk)
ISBN: 978-0-367-14209-4 (Volume 2) (pbk)
ISBN: 978-0-429-03074-1 (Volume 2) (ebk)

Publisher's Note
The publisher has gone to great lengths to ensure the quality of this reprint but points out that some imperfections in the original copies may be apparent.

Disclaimer
The publisher has made every effort to trace copyright holders and would welcome correspondence from those they have been unable to trace.

To Judith, and to Daniel and Helen

Religious Education 5–12

Derek Bastide

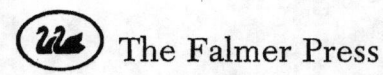 The Falmer Press
(A Member of the Taylor & Francis Group)
London, New York and Philadelphia

UK   The Falmer Press, Falmer House, Barcombe, Lewes, East Sussex, BN8 5DL

USA   The Falmer Press, Taylor & Francis Inc., 242 Cherry Street, Philadelphia, PA 19106-1906

© 1987 D. Bastide

All rights reserved. No part of this publication may be reproduced, stored in a retrieval system, or transmitted in any form or by any means, electronic, mechanical, photocopying, recording or otherwise, without permission in writing from the Publisher.

First published 1987

Library of Congress Cataloguing in Publication Data is available on request

ISBN 1-85000-149-9
ISBN 1-85000-150-2 (pbk.)

Jacket design by Caroline Archer

Typeset in 11/13 Caledonia by
Imago Publishing Ltd, Thame, Oxon

Printed in Great Britain by Taylor & Francis (Printers) Ltd, Basingstoke

Contents

Acknowledgements		vi
Chapter 1	Introduction	1
Chapter 2	What Are We Trying To Do: Some Aims and Objectives	6
Chapter 3	Children and Religion: Age and Understanding	16
Chapter 4	What Do We Mean By Religion?	24
Chapter 5	An Implicit Approach Through Themes	35
Chapter 6	An Introduction to Five Religions	50
Chapter 7	Teaching World Religions	79
Chapter 8	An Extended Topic: Pilgrimage	88
Chapter 9	Christian Festivals	99
Chapter 10	Teaching Festivals	108
Chapter 11	The Bible	115
Chapter 12	An Approach Through Bible Background	119
Chapter 13	Understanding the Bible	124
Chapter 14	Teaching About Jesus	139
Chapter 15	An Extended Topic: The Dead Sea Scrolls and Masada	151
Chapter 16	Belief in Action	164
Chapter 17	Resources	170
Index		194

Acknowledgements

Anyone who produces a book of this nature is in debt to various groups of people: to colleagues of all persuasions who over a number of years have shared ideas; to children whom one has taught and who have taught so much in return; to one's students who have both questioned and been prepared to experiment. I am very grateful to them all.

I am also immensely appreciative of the understanding support of my family and also of the unfailingly efficient work of Joyce Clark who typed the manuscript.

1 Introduction

It is very easy for class teachers to feel out of date! New and exciting but dimly perceived areas such as micro-computing and craft design technology are rapidly developing in schools. This increase in the *breadth* of the curriculum necessarily puts additional strain upon the teacher. However, it is not just the addition of new elements which puts on the pressure; it is not only a question of new areas but of new ways in old ones — new approaches to the teaching of reading, of mathematics, science and so on.

Very few areas of the curriculum have experienced changes in quite the same way as religious education. Revolution is a not infrequent way of describing it. In twenty years, religious education has come down from the pulpit and now sits at the cross roads of a multicultural society. Its aims have undergone a radical transformation and its subject content has inevitably shown a considerable shift. The role of religious education which has been emerging gradually has been confirmed officially by the Swann Report, *Education for All* (1985), which has made it, in school terms, a central plank in the bridge of understanding between the various ethnic groups in the country.

In the past twenty years, therefore, religious education has gradually changed its *role* and this implies a change too in its *aims* and to an extent in its *content*. Teachers, caught up in the middle of this, are puzzled by it. Some are not interested and have no intention of teaching it. The evidence suggests, though, that most are unsure about what religious education is trying to do in the school and feel guilty about their ignorance. A teacher put it down bluntly but succinctly.

> I used to know what to do. I know it has all changed now but I'm not really sure in what way. I know that there's a lot

more world religions in it now but I can't say that I'm very familiar with them. That all leaves me not really knowing what to do!

It is this situation which this book seeks to address. It is for all teachers and students in training for teaching (and, of course, for all those interested in the area) who want to offer the best they can in religious education but who are not sure what they ought to be doing and for whom much of the subject content is unfamiliar. The book attempts to deal with both prongs of this need — both the need for help with subject content as well as with approaches in the classroom.

New approaches to religious education do involve children looking beyond the traditional Christian content of RE and thus puts the teacher in interesting but often unfamiliar territory. A definite attempt has been made to provide teachers with information for them to use, principally about a number of world religions (Christianity, Hinduism, Islam, Judaism and Sikhism), on Christian festivals and on some aspects of the Bible. It would be misleading to make false claims about this information. To try to deal adequately with, say, Islam, in 2–3000 words, even by focussing on those dimensions which would be most suitable for children, is an impossibility. It is intended to be a first stage of finding out, a plotting out of the area which can lead the teacher easily to follow it up in one of the books listed in the resources' section.

Teachers do need, and also feel the need, for some information and understanding of religion and religions if they are going to work successfully in religious education. They also need an understanding of how to approach it in the classroom — and this involves an interrelationship of the *aims* of the subject, the *age, stage* and *experience* of the children and the *subject content*. The first three chapters focus upon the meaning of religion, children's understanding of religion and a consideration of the aims and objectives of the subject.

The approach of the book is essentially *practical*. It seeks to tie down both aims and subject material into specific schemes of work — but without falling into the trap of trying to provide a blue print. The British educational system has fostered a tradition of teacher individuality for too long for this to be successful! What it does is to provide practical assistance in two ways:

   (i) through topic schemes of work laid out with aims and an outline of possible approaches or of the general development of the subject content;

(ii) through detailed accounts recording experiences of successful religious education work done in school.

In this way it is intended to provide a firm framework of structure with enough room for teachers to use their own professional judgment and their own best ways of working. Two of the topic schemes are extended themes, one (Pilgrimage) from a world religion base and the other (Masada and the Dead Sea Scrolls) from a Biblical base, which look in detail both at the subject content for the teacher and also at ways in which the work could be approached in the classroom.

Anyone who looks at the teaching of religious education will inevitably notice considerable variations in practice. It therefore seems sensible to outline the approach of this book *before* it is read.

First of all, it assumes that religious education in school is different from religious nurture which is the work and privilege of the appropriate religious community.

The underlying view is that the study of religion in school should aim at all levels at fostering an *understanding* of religion along with the related attitudes of *respect* and *empathy*. Understanding, like conceptual thinking, is developmental and teachers would expect different levels of understanding at five years and at twelve years of age. The teacher should nevertheless aim at encouraging understanding at whatever level. It goes without saying that teachers should select subject content which assists the overall development of understanding, respect and empathy.

As this is the overriding aim there is a sense in which content is less important than intention. If we are to try to judge success in our religious education teaching, then we would probably be much more satisfied if our children had some feeling for awe and mystery or had some understanding of a pilgrim's feelings in Jerusalem or Mecca than if they could (only) recite the names and dates of the Ten Gurus of Sikhism. This is not to denigrate subject content or information. While it is possible to have information without understanding, it is never possible to have understanding without some facts; you cannot understand in a vacuum. In order for anyone to understand anything of the pilgrim's feelings in Jerusalem or Mecca they have to know something of what happened and happens there that gives the places their significance. However this point is being emphasized to make the distinction that in the end religious education is not about knowing lots of facts about religions but about developing a sympathetic understanding of them.

That is the essential approach to religious education and that will determine the sort of content that a teacher might select but still leaves considerable flexibility for the interests and styles of different teachers. There are however four more assumptions in the book which determine its approach.

(i) Children should be introduced to some degree to a number of religions. In this book the focus has been placed on those religions which flourish in Britain and which have considerable numbers of followers. It is significant to note that there are now numerically more Muslims than Methodists here. Hence the emphasis is upon Hinduism, Islam, Judaism and Sikhism as well as upon Christianity. All children, it is advocated, should be given the opportunity of some learning contact with a number of religions.

(ii) The experience of religion for the overwhelming number of children in Britain is Christian and so it would be expected that for most children, certainly in the younger years, the majority of their religious education would be concerned with Christianity. It may well be that in the multiracial schools there could be a policy of equal time for each religion but this would not be the norm in most schools.

(iii) Religion should be presented to children as a *living activity*: *activity* because it is to these aspects of religion which the children we are concerned with relate most readily and *living* because they are not dead relics of a past age. There has been a danger that religious education has tended to focus almost exclusively upon the past and this is well illustrated by its earlier concentration on Bible stories. The story dimension of religions *is* important but it needs to be placed alongside areas which are concerned with what it means to be a religious adherent today — festivals, worship, communities, stories of people living out their faith.

(iv) It is very important with the youngest children to lay the right foundations and it may well be necessary for the teacher of these years to work without the security of much explicit or conventional religious material. There is a danger of introducing material too early and it is at this level that teachers find that they have to make the hardest decisions. This is considered further in Chapter 5.

The book focusses upon five complementary approaches to religious education: thematic work, world religions, Christian festivals, the

Introduction

Bible and biography. Of these the strongest emphasis has been placed upon two — world religions and the Bible — because it is around these that teachers express most concern. Approaching RE through world religions is seen by very many teachers as a new and exciting development but one which is largely unfamiliar to them. How can they introduce it into their classroom? The Bible, for so long almost the text book of RE, will remain for very many teachers the central element in their religious education work. They are often only too aware of the sorts of difficulties which Goldman pinpointed but still wish to devise more suitable ways of using Biblical material in their classrooms. These are very pressing concerns for very many and this book attempts to offer ways of proceeding.

The aim of the book is to present a framework rather than a straitjacket. There are undergirding aims but there is still sufficient flexibility to a teacher to open the RE wardrobe and to select items which both provide a coordinated outfit but also which is suited to the teacher, the situation and the children.

2 What Are We Trying To Do: Some Aims and Objectives

A number of primary school teachers attending courses at a teachers' centre were asked the following question: 'What do you think ought to be the aim of religious education in school?' Here is a sample of their replies.

(a) To get the children to know something about God. Hardly any of them seem to go to Sunday school these days so it's the only opportunity they'll have to learn about Him.
(b) I don't know. I never teach it myself. I'm not religious.
(c) To give the kids some knowledge of their religious background. After all they've got to know something to understand Milton and Shakespeare.
(d) To help the children to have some understanding of how other people live and what they believe. To make them more tolerant I suppose.
(e) To make children Christian.
(f) To make children better behaved, I guess — though it doesn't seem to work!

It is this wide range of answer which shows how much confusion there is about the aims of RE. Views certainly do differ though it is possible to detect three broad — and differing — approaches:

(i) the 'confessional' approach;
(ii) the 'giving them the facts' approach;
(iii) the 'understanding religion' approach.

Briefly, these mean:

The 'confessional' approach sees the aim of religious education as leading pupils into Christian commitment — replies (a) and (e) above fit neatly into this approach. This approach assumes the truth of the

What Are We Trying To Do: Some Aims and Objectives

Christian religion and would seek to initiate pupils into it over the period of compulsory education. In practice, this aim is little different from that of the Church or the Sunday school. Sometimes it has been called the 'missionary' approach. It is interesting that reply (b) might also subscribe to this view of the aims of religious education — although she does not agree with it!

The 'giving them the facts' approach rejects completely the 'confessional' approach with its desire to teach children to be Christians. It adopts a completely neutral view of whether religions are true or false; they are around and children ought to know about them. Reply (c) above fits well into this approach.

The 'understanding religion' approach rejects both these approaches. It starts from an uncommitted position but does not feel that just giving children information is sufficient. Children need to be helped to understand religion. Reply (d) fits partly into this approach.

How Did All This Come About?

Historically in England there has always been a close link between school and church. Most schools before 1870, the date when compulsory education for all was agreed, were founded by religious bodies and transmitted their religious teaching. Most of the schools built as a result of the 1870 Act continued the practice of giving religious instruction although of a non denominational kind. In the 1944 Butler Education Act, when religious instruction was made compulsory, it was only making mandatory what was universal practice.

The 1944 Education Act required the following with regard to religion:

(i) that religious instruction should be given in every county school;
(ii) that each day should begin with an act of worship;
(iii) that there should be a right of withdrawal for both pupils and teachers on the grounds of conscience;
(iv) that each local education authority should formulate its agreed syllabus for religious instruction (or adapt that of another authority).

This clearly implied a 'confessional' approach to religious teaching. The name of the subject, religious *instruction*, the daily act of worship, the provision for parents to withdraw their children from both the teaching and the worship and of non-believing teachers to refuse to enter into this part of the curriculum on the grounds of conscience all showed that what the Act intended was that children should be inducted into the Christian religion. Agreed syllabuses, written at this time, make this abundantly clear. Here is an example from the Surrey Syllabus of 1945:

> The aim of the syllabus is to secure that children attending the schools of the County ... may gain knowledge of the common Christian faith held by their fathers for nearly 2000 years; may seek for themselves in Christianity principles which give a purpose to life and a guide to all its problems, and may find inspiration, power and courage to work for their own welfare, for that of their fellow creatures and for the growth of God's Kingdom.

This approach to religious teaching reflected the sort of society at the time. Most people identified in some way and at some level with the Christian religion. A large majority turned to the churches for the rites of passage — for baptism, for marriage and for burial, though the majority were not regular church attenders. There were, of course, groups within society which clearly rejected the Christian religion, bodies like the British Humanist Association and the National Secular Society. They were persistent campaigners for the removal of this sort of religious teaching from the schools but they made little headway with the vast majority of parents and teachers.

However changes were afoot both in school and in society. During the 1950s and 1960s there was immigration into Britain on a large scale from the Caribbean, Africa, Cyprus and from the Indian sub-continent. Practically all those from India and Pakistan practised religions other than Christianity. Mosques began to appear in Bradford, Hindu temples in Manchester and Gurdwaras (Sikh temples) in Middlesex. These new residents had children who attended local schools alongside indigenous children and it was not unusual in many of our cities for a teacher in a primary school to find that she had within her class adherents of four or more religions.

This, of course, raised the question of whether it was right given a class containing practising Muslims, Sikhs and Hindus to present Christianity as *the* religion. Some people saw no problem but many others did.

In a wider way too within the general population there were changes taking place — attitudes towards Christianity were changing. The 1960s saw a rapid decline in church attendance. People felt freer about admitting religious doubt — certainly in public opinion polls on religious allegiance the number of professed agnostics and atheists increased. The change was inevitably reflected in the teaching profession and a number of teachers felt unable to teach religious education in this way: 'How can I teach RE if I don't believe in God — it would make me a hypocrite'.

Within schools, too, there were changes. Visitors walking round primary classrooms noticed that teachers spent less time standing in front of their classes and talking to them and more time moving round the children as they worked. Children were being encouraged to learn from practical activity, to discover things for themselves. In mathematics they were being encouraged to attempt to solve problems, in creative writing to express themselves through poetry and story. Above all they were being encouraged not to accept things merely on authority but to question and then to challenge and to think for themselves. The confessional approach to RE did not seem to fit in. Although religious education as it was conceived seemed to be very much out of joint, there were still persistent and massive demands for its continued presence in schools. In surveys of parental opinion, around 90 per cent were in favour of RE in schools. Commentators put it down to many causes — guilt, a desire to offload on to the school an unpalatable part of parenthood (rather like sex education), a feeling that it might encourage good behaviour. Whatever the reasons the demand still seemed to be there.

All this led many of those involved in religious education to seek out a different approach. Religion would still figure in the school curriculum but its *aims* would be different.

One which appeared attractive to many was the straightforward 'giving them the facts' approach. The argument for it goes thus: children live in a world surrounded by religion: the church on the corner, brothers and sisters baptised, aunts and uncles married, monarchs crowned, the Bible permeating much of literature. They need to know all about this as part of understanding how the world works. This can be developed: on their TV screens children see and hear about mosques, Muslims, Sikhs in turbans and so on. They should have some knowledge of other religions and ways of living so as to enlarge their understanding of the world — and with some luck — learn greater tolerance through knowledge. The teachers' role is clearly not to foster belief or to encourage commitment to any particular religion nor even to commend a religious view as opposed to a non-religious view of life. They are there to provide information that will help the child to make more sense of the world in which he/she lives.

On first sight this view seems ideal. It respects the plurality of society; it is seen by most people as a valuable exercise; teachers of any religious persuasion or of none can teach it without conflict of conscience. They can make statements like 'Christians *believe* that Jesus is the Son of God' or 'Muslims *believe* that the Koran is the Word of God' — factual statements which any teacher can convey to any class of children — they are not required to evaluate them or to examine them for truth.

It was this very openness and neutrality, this insistence upon keeping to the *facts about* religion, to being always descriptive that led to numbers of people being unhappy about this approach to the teaching of religion. It would be likened to certain approaches to the teaching of music, in which pupils learn about the lives of great composers, the name of every musical instrument, where each one is positioned in the orchestra but never hear a symphony or make a note of their own music. In what sense could this approach be called a musical education? In the same way the 'giving them the facts' approach to religious education was seen as arid and as avoiding the heart of the subject. There was no real place for *appreciation* or *understanding*.

Advocates of the third approach, that of *'understanding religion'* reject both the confessional and the 'giving them the facts' approaches, the confessional on the grounds that they do not want to persuade children to commit themselves to a particular religious stance and the 'giving them the facts' approach because it avoids the central questions of religion. The key term they use is to 'understand' and by understand they mean to empathize. They want, as far as is possible, to get children to step into the shoes of other people and to see things from their standpoint. So, understanding in this sense involves appreciation. For example, it is a fact that devout Muslims fast during the hours of daylight in the month of Ramadan. Children can be told this as a simple fact but if they are to have some understanding of it they need to have some glimmering of *why* devout Muslims fast. In this way they can begin, even if only in a very small way, to enter inside a religion. In this sense it is often said that religious education should transcend the informative.

Alongside this emphasis of looking with sensitivity at religions, and to a small extent from within them, comes the notion of *personal search*. This underlines the idea that children (and many adults too for that matter) are on a personal quest for meaning, trying to make sense of such insistent questions as 'Is this all there is to life or is there more?' or 'What happens when we are dead?'. It is to these deeper

What Are We Trying To Do: Some Aims and Objectives

questions that religions address themselves and this approach to religious education can be helpful in this personal search. It might be argued that this is more a concern for the teenager than for the 5-year-old or the 9-year-old. As an emphasis this is almost certainly true but it would be a mistake to overlook younger children's less sophisticated attempts to make sense of some of these religious questions for themselves.

This approach is reflected in a number of influential publications. *The Fourth R* (the Church of England Commission on Religious Education in Schools, usually referred to as the 'Durham Report') states:

> The aim of religious education should be to explore the place and significance of religion in human life and so to make a distinctive contribution to each pupil's search for a faith by which to live ... The teacher is thus seeking rather to initiate his pupils into knowledge which he encourages them to explore and appreciate, than into a system which he requires them to accept. To press for acceptance of a particular faith or belief system is the duty and the privilege of the churches and other similar religious bodies. It is certainly not the task of the teacher in a county school. If the teacher is to press for any conversion, it is conversion from a shallow and unreflective attitude to life. If he is to press for commitment, it is commitment to the religious quest, to that search for meaning, purpose and value which is open to all men. (p. 103)

Discovering an Approach, (The Schools' Council Project on Religious Education in Primary Schools) indicates that:

> Religious education can build upon the desire to make sense of life. It tries to help pupils to enter imaginatively into the experience of a believer so that they can appreciate the importance to him of what he believes and does. It can provide a basis of understanding and appreciation upon which reasoned assessments and informed decisions can be made. In short, religious education is helping pupils to understand religion. However, such an understanding is not quickly acquired; for many it is a life-long process. So, in the primary school, teachers are concerned with laying foundations, with the question of the extent to which we can equip children with the tools of understanding.

Religious Education 5-12

Some Initial Implications

To make the adjustment from thinking of religious education as teaching Christianity to thinking of religious education as helping children to understand religion can be difficult for both believers and unbelievers. It makes teachers examine their attitudes to religion and the religious education and it raises the question of the status of Christianity with these changed aims.

There are some who say that if religious education is going to move genuinely in the direction of helping children to understand religion then logic demands that no one religion should be given any special prominence. 'Fair do's for all' would be the slogan. It can be agreed that as Britain moves into a multi-faith society — after all since the early 1980s there have been more Muslims than Methodists on these islands — this principle becomes more important.

However, against this, there do seem to be strong social and educational reasons for giving special attention to Christianity in religious education.

Western civilization, including Britain, has been, and in many ways still is, influenced very strongly by Christianity. Our art, music, drama, poetry, literature, customs, traditions, even many of our swear terms, arise out of and are shaped by Christianity. It may well be that a fair proportion of the population has rejected personal commitment to Christianity as a religion and the large majority has ceased to worship publicly in any serious way, but it can still be argued that Britain is a Christian culture.

From the young child's viewpoint, experience of religion tends to be of Christianity. We decorate our shop windows, with, among other things, angels at Christmastime, we have pancakes on Shrove Tuesday, eat hot cross buns on Good Friday, receive and give Easter eggs on Easter Day. Children hear terms like, God, Jesus, saying prayers and, while they may but dimly understand them, use them. Christianity is part of their mental furniture.

If religious education, like the rest of the primary curriculum is going to build on and extend existing experience and understanding, it seems inevitable that much of the content will be drawn from Christianity: this is not to present Christianity as the true religion but to use it as the obvious vehicle for starting children off on the task of beginning to understand what religion is all about.

Three provisos should be added to this:

(i) this does not preclude in any way the introduction of

material drawn from other religious traditions, even with very young children;
(ii) as the child develops, the amount of material from other religious traditions is very likely to increase;
(iii) where the children being taught live in a multi faith area, where there are, for example, Hindu temples or Mosques in the local environment, this will affect their normal experience of religion and mean that the content of the religious education in the primary schools will be more variegated than for those living perhaps in Windermere or Ramsgate or Lewes.

It is important to remember, though, that although in terms of syllabus *content* Christianity will be dominant, the younger the child the more so, the *aim* and *approach* is changing. It is the role of the church to proclaim and to teach its faith. The process of the education of the young within the church is often now called *'Christian nurture'* to distinguish it from the *religious education* of the school. The way that the school uses Christian material will be different; there may be considerable overlap in the *content* of religious teaching in both church and school but the goal will not be the same.

Some Objectives for Religious Education with Children aged 5 to 12 Years

So far in this chapter discussion has been in the area of general aims. Objectives arise out of the general aims and provide much more specific starting points for teachers. A summary of the general aims would be:

(i) that religious education in schools is concerned more with understanding and appreciation than in commending belief in any specific religion;
(ii) that religious education is concerned with helping children in their personal search for meaning;
(iii) that in schools where there are no children from non-Christian ethnic minority groups Christianity will be the major focus of study though material from other religious traditions will also be included, increasingly as the children get older.

Religious Education 5–12

In schools where there are different religions represented among the children then the balance will be different.
The following objectives could be helpful:

(i) to foster in children feelings of mystery, wonder and joy and a sense of interrelatedness with other people;

(ii) to encourage and help children to recognize and respond to questions about meaning and value as appropriate to their age and stage and to assist them in the process of their personal search for meaning;

(iii) to help children to face and to come to terms with difficult and painful situations they encounter;

(iv) to do everything possible to help children to understand and respect other people, their beliefs and their cultural differences.

(v) to provide children with knowledge of the lives of the founders and the significant figures (including modern ones) in different religious traditions;

(vi) to help children to have some awareness of the significance of festivals within religious practice and to have some knowledge of the stories which underly the major Christian festivals and of festivals from other religious traditions;

(vii) to assist children to have some familiarity with places of worship and of the forms of worship which take place within them, if possible at first hand;

(viii) to introduce children to the sacred books of different religions;

(ix) to provide children with the opportunity of developing some awareness of the use, for example, of myth, symbol, simile and metaphor in religious language;

(x) to enable children to gain some understanding of the Bible with especial reference to its composition, its literature and the world which it reflects.

These objectives are by no means exhaustive. Some teachers would want to subtract some and others would want to add more. Clearly, much will depend upon the age of the child although most of these objections would be relevant for 6-year-olds as well as 11-year-olds though the specific content would vary considerably, for example: objective (vi) is concerned with festivals; both 6-year-olds and 11-year-olds will study Christmas though the older children's study will be different (hopefully) both in approach and content from the work of the younger age group.

What Are We Trying To Do: Some Aims and Objectives

It will be noted that the first four objectives are different from the remaining six. The final six concerned explicit religious material; the first four are much more general and would arise from many different situations in the classroom.

These objectives will be behind much of the choice of content in this book. A school's selection of topics would normally be done in such a way that all the objectives would be covered so that the pupils were presented with a view of religion which is both broad and balanced.

3 Children and Religion: Age and Understanding

At the heart of the educational process is the child, or so most teachers would argue. I can remember, as my first day at a new school, hearing from the cleaner about the teacher, just retired, whose class of first year juniors I was taking over. 'Oh, he was a wonderful teacher. He used to talk to the children all day about Africa and all those distant places. It was way over their heads but he knew so much'. Most teachers would disassociate themselves from her verdict! It is an accepted axiom that teachers should match material to the age and stage of the child. We would not expect 5-year-olds to embark on calculus nor 8-year-olds to make a systematic study of Shakespeare's plays. It might, of course, be appropriate for the exceptional child but it will not happen very often!

It is often quite surprising that some teachers who would agree wholeheartedly with all this, ignore it completely when it comes to religious education. I once witnessed a teacher of very young children, excellent in every way, teaching her 4-year-olds about the Christian doctrine of the Trinity. She was using visual devices which provided examples of things which were both three and one at the same time, such as triangles and the clover leaf. At the end of the session the children were able to use the right words: Father, Son and Holy Spirit, Three and One and so on. Lovely on the surface perhaps, but one may wonder what the children really made of it.

This separation of religion from the rest of the curriculum in terms of children's understanding is odd but persistent. For over a century now writers on religious education have been urging teachers to think about the suitability of their teaching materials for the capacities of their pupils. It was not until the 1960s that Ronald Goldman undertook substantial research into the development of children's religious understanding which he published in 1964 in his book, *Religious*

Thinking from Childhood to Adolescence. In 1965 he wrote a second book *Readiness for Religion* which attempted to interpret some of his findings for teachers and to consider implications for religious education particularly in the primary school.

Goldman was motivated by a deep and long term concern about the effectiveness of RE in schools and about the misunderstandings which formed in children's minds which were not dissipated. On a comparatively trivial level there are the howlers, arising from using unfamiliar language, which children make and which parents and teachers love to repeat: Pontius the Pilot with his aeroplane, Our Father which art in Heaven, Harold be thy name ... lead us not into Thames Station, and so on. These are occasioned by children trying to make sense of unfamiliar words. At a deeper level children hear stories from the Bible and try to make sense of them in terms of their own experience. Violet Madge tells of Miles, fresh from a holiday in Blackpool, who heard at school a story of Jesus telling a story from a boat. In his drawing of the incident which he entitles 'Jesus talking to people on the sands at Blackpool' he paints Blackpool Tower in the background and an aeroplane flying overhead.[1] Deeper still Damian (8:3) on hearing the story of Abraham's attempt to sacrifice his son, Isaac, concluded 'Both God and Abraham are really horrible. I'm glad I wasn't Isaac'. Many teachers over the years have noted all these misunderstandings and many more and found them amusing but at the same time worrying.

How extensive is this misunderstanding? Does it remain or is it at some point unravelled?

Goldman's Research Method

Goldman interviewed 200 children aged between 6 and 15+ years. He showed three pictures: a child entering a church with adults, a child praying alone and a child looking at a mutilated Bible. He told three stories: Moses and the Burning Bush, Moses and the Crossing of the Red Sea and the Temptations of Jesus in the Wilderness. Both the pictures and the stories were carefully chosen after a number of pilot experiments.

Religious Education 5–12

Goldman's Findings

Goldman found (like Piaget's general theory) that children's ability to think and understand religious concepts developed in a series of stages.

Piaget posits five stages:

    (i)   sensori-motor stage (birth to 18 months/2 years);
    (ii) preconceptual stage (18 months to 4/5 years);
   (iii) intuitive stage (4/5 to 7 years);
   (iv) concrete operational stage (7 years to 11/12 years);
    (v) formal operational stage (11/12 years onwards).

(*NB* all ages are mental ages, not chronological ages)
Goldman found that children's understanding of religious concepts followed the same pattern but with two variations:

    (i)   he discerned intermediate stages;
    (ii) he found that the concrete operational stage lasted longer, until about the mental age of 13 or 14.

Linking his research on the development of children's religious thinking, with the limitations children also have in language and in experience, he posited five stages of development in religious thinking (again all ages are mental ages):

    (i)   pre-religious thought (up to 7/8);
    (ii) sub-religious thought 1 (7/9);
   (iii) sub-religious thought 2 (9/11);
   (iv) personal religious thought 1 (11/13);
    (v) personal religious thought 2 (13+).

For the primary school teacher the first three stages are of most significance and Goldman spent a considerable amount of time defining the characteristics of each stage.

Pre-Religious Thought (up to 7/8 years) — Infant School

At this stage children's thinking generally is marked by two main features: egocentricity and monofocalism. Egocentricity means that children's judgments are made solely from their own standpoint. They are not able to stand in other people's shoes and see it from their viewpoint. For example, when children at this stage were asked 'Why was Moses afraid to look on God' one answer was 'God had a beard and

Children and Religion: Age and Understanding

Moses did not like beards'! Monofocal thinking means that children pick out a feature of an event, not necessarily an important feature, and generalize from it and hence make mistakes because they can't as yet reverse their thinking. The particular marks of religious thinking are:

(i) Religious ideas from part of a fairytale world in which God operates alongside Father Christmas, elves and goblins.

(ii) God is seen in very human-like terms, usually wearing Palestinian dress, for example 'a long sort of white shawl'. There is clearly considerable confusion about God: he lives in the sky and he's here too but he doesn't come here very often ... Goldman collected a number of quotations made by young children in his samples:

God is the man in the moon. He has a round head and he has bent ears. He lives in a round home.

I think God might live up in space but I don't know. I think he might clean up his house sometimes. I think he might eat something like bread and sausages when he is hungry.

God is in the sky and you can't see him. He flies around. Sometimes he stops behind a cloud to have something to eat. He goes down to land at night to see shepherds and talk to them.

These comments reveal a variety of thinking, of fantasy and physical matters blended together. (*Readiness for Religion*, p. 80)

(iii) The Bible is seen as a very special book. Caroline, one of Goldman's sample, said that it was 'dictated by God and Jesus took it down on his typewriter'. Because it is believed to come from God it partakes of his qualities and is therefore invested with great awe. It is, of course, seen as completely and literally true.

(iv) Prayer is very egocentric and magical. There is also no problem about unanswered prayer because 'they all come true', though sometimes 'a boy who has been naughty or has not said please won't get anything'.

(v) Many religious words are used which are not understood. The unwary can sometimes be mislead about a child's understanding of much religious material by listening to his facility with religious language.

Religious Education 5-12

Sub Religious Thought 1 (7/9 years)

In this stage the children have moved into operational thinking and have achieved levels of concrete thinking. They are much more able to relate facts together, to classify experience and to generalize. Thinking is much less monofocal: rarely now will the child select a peripheral feature of an event and generalize from it. Egocentricity, while still present, is much less pervasive. A much more likely response to the question, 'Why was Moses afraid to look on God' at this stage is 'It might have been because the bright light from the bush was frightening him' (p. 118).

The particular marks of religious thinking are:

(i) the fairytale world, so alive to very young children, is receding rapidly. The 8-year-old now knows that Father Christmas is only his father dressed up!

(ii) Children's concrete thinking has the advantage of making their understanding of religious ideas much less fanciful and idiosyncratic. It also has the effect of causing the child to interpret religious ideas which are often abstract and symbolic in literal and physical terms. When questioned about what Jesus meant when he said 'Man shall not live by bread alone', a common answer at this stage: 'you should eat something else with it — like butter' (MA 10.1)! Here you have the logic of the children trying to puzzle out the meaning of Jesus' cryptic reply but still missing the point because they are locked in a concrete way of thinking.

(iii) The picture of God is still superhuman rather than supernatural. He is still Palestinian and living in the sky and making occasional visits to the world. God remains powerful but still unpredictable.

(iv) The Bible is still seen as having been written by God and therefore literally true though greater experience and understanding of the world would lead to a rejection of Caroline's notion that Jesus took it down on his typewriter! Understanding of stories within the Bible is more logical and less idiosyncratic though, as was noted in (ii) above, most of the abstract concepts in the Bible are missed by the children.

Sub Religious Thought II (9/12 years+)

Children in this stage are still in Piaget's concrete operational stage and therefore, any of their attempts to interpret and understand religious concepts are hampered by this concrete nature of their thinking. In fact, Goldman's research led him to believe that concrete thinking predominated in the understanding of religious material until the mental age of 13.

(i) Goldman felt that the quality of thinking about God could be described as a move from a super human to a supernatural, though literalisms still persist. There is evidence of considerable thought on the part of many children of this age especially in trying to reconcile apparent impossibilities (at least from a concrete perspective) such as the notion of God being everywhere and yet in specific places at the same time. Abstract thinking may resolve this by perceiving God as a spirit but this does not come easily to concrete thinking. It is interesting that children of this age often represent God in picture form with the normal human shape but with a number of arms stretching out from the body; this is also one way of coming to terms with prayers which intercede for groups of people in different parts of the world.

(ii) Goldman detected the beginnings of what he called a *dualistic* view of life, by which he meant a tendency in the child to draw a distinction between the *world of religion* and *real world*. The world of religion can be seen as being *holy*: 'holy people living in holy houses in the holy land' (MA 9:7); the real world is the one we live in. The world of religion is characterized by the Bible — a book of long ago, where miracles happened, where God came and went. In the real world miracles are not seen as happening in the same way, nor does God appear to come and go in the same way. Goldman noted that many children believe in both worlds at the same time but for many it is the beginning of a process which will lead to the rejection of the world of religion. For some too it will come quite early: the 9-year-old child (MA 10:5) who put aside the reference book he was reading and asked his teacher which was the true explanation of the origin of life, evolution or the story of Adam and Eve is at the crossroads.

Goldman pursued his research right through to young people of

15+ years and identified and described stages of thinking beyond this but these will not be dealt with here as they are not of direct relevance to the teacher of children in this age range.

Goldman's work had a tremendous impact in the 1960s being received by some with relief and by others with anger. Some church people, especially those who interpreted the Bible in a literal fashion, reacted unfavourably. Some psychologists questioned some of his methods. Nonetheless it had made for considerable changes in the way schools, particularly primary schools, approached the teaching of religious education. Writing in 1977, the American psychologist, John H. Peatling, who has himself done extensive work in the study of developing religious understanding, concluded:

> Basically, Goldman was right: children and adolescents do become increasingly abstract in their religious thinking. However, Goldman and Piaget are wrong, if one reads either of them in such a way that the transition from a concrete stage to an abstract stage of thinking is presumed to be rapid (or, even quasi-instantaneous).[2]

Peatling sees Goldman's work as seminal and that subsequent research will inevitably refine different parts of it. This is as it should be.

So what implications does Goldman's work have for primary school teachers? Below are four points some of which are closely interrelated.

1. Goldman points quite clearly to the fact that children's understanding of religious concepts *develops*. This is recognized by teachers in all other areas of the curriculum but often there was this exception made of religion.
2. If children's understanding of religious concepts develops so teachers must see RE developmentally and ask questions about the suitability and appropriateness of teaching material for the age group in question.
   Are the parables of Jesus suitable for 5-year-olds? Is the Eightfold Path of Buddhism appropriate for 9-year-olds?
3. Teachers must be more aware of what is going on in the children's minds. Are we setting up all sorts of misunderstandings? The sacrifice of Isaac may be a dramatic and moving story but what ideas about God are we implementing in young minds? Do the miracle stories of Jesus help children to see him in the way the Gospel writers intended to portray him or does he appear as a 'magic man'?

4 Is our teaching helpful to the development of religious understanding? To use Grimmit's terminology are we providing helpful *stepping stones* rather than *stumbling blocks*.³

Notes

1 MADGE, V. (1971) *Introducing Young Children to Jesus*, SCM Press
2 PEATLING J. H. (1977) *Learning for Living*, 16, 3, Spring.
3 GRIMMIT M. (1978) *What can I do in R.E.?*, Mayhew McCrimmon, p. 47

4 What Do We Mean By Religion?

Defining religion is no easy task. A group of students offered the following definitions:

(a) It's trying to lead a good life (8 replies)
(b) It's believing in God (6)
(c) It's believing in the supernatural (1)
(d) It's a form of mental illness (1)
(e) It's the opiate of the people (1)
(f) It's going to church (or to the Temple) (3)

Here there is a variety of views four of which attempt to be definitions. Two of them are not: (d) is a psychological assessment and (e) is a comment on the function of religion in society, borrowed from Karl Marx. Of the four definitions offered, there could easily be concerns about adequacy. Religion certainly *is* about trying to lead a good life but is it not also about believing in certain things too? Religion is very difficult to fit into succinct definitions.

The following two approaches to the matter can be helpful:

(i) religion as a personal search for meaning, and value;
(ii) religion as a six dimensional activity.

Religion as a Personal Search for Meaning and Value

This is an approach which sees religion principally as an individual's, or as a group's, attempt to make sense of experience. Underlying this is the notion that there are certain fundamental questions which certainly puzzle most people and which often also baffle and distress. These questions would include 'Why are we here?', 'Is there a purpose in life?', 'Is death the end?', 'How can I to know what is right?', 'To what

What Do We Mean By Religion?

extent am I responsible to other people?' and so on. These interrelated questions are ones which most people ask at certain points in their lives and attempt to provide answers to them. Religions tend to fulfil this function as they do give a coherent answer to these insistent questions though they may not always be identical answers. In traditional societies where there is little change over generations and where there is a widely-held religion, then it is likely that the young will be inducted into that religion and imbibe the answers without necessarily asking the fundamental questions listed above. In a society too, such as that in the Soviet Union, where there is an officially promulgated and widely accepted philosophy, then it is likely that young people will be nurtured in that so that it becomes part of them and begins to shape their thoughts. In a society like Britain where there is a variety of options, Christian and non-Christian, agnostic and atheist, then it is much more likely that young people will have to engage in their own search for meaning.

This approach to religion inevitably raises objections, notably:

1. A number of believers from different religious traditions would be loathe to see their religions from this angle. For very many (if not most) Muslims, Islam's truth comes from the revelation of God. People, they would agree, would know little of God if he had not chosen to reveal himself through Mohammed and through the Koran. It is this revelation which demands faith. Very many Christians would adopt a similar stance: that Jesus Christ is the vehicle for God's fullest revelation of himself and the Bible bears record to this. To see religion as a search for meaning would seem to place too much emphasis upon the individual and not enough upon God who out of loving kindness has shown something of himself and of his ways to the human race.

2. Seeing religion as a search for meaning, could seem to imply that any form of meaning could be termed 'religion'. What, for example, should be said of Marxism which is certainly a framework for seeing meaning in human history and in the fulfilment of the human race. Marxism sees history as moving towards a goal, towards the victory of the proletariat and the eventual disappearance of the state in the perfect society. This provides answers to the fundamental questions and they form a coherent system. In the definition of religion as being a search for meaning then Marxism could be seen as a religion. The same point could be made for Humanism. Again, Humanism is a faith system which gives answers to the fundamental ques-

tions and provides a framework for meaning. Yet to call both Marxism and Humanism religions is likely to enrage both Marxists and Humanists who normally regard themselves as people who have rejected religion! It also seems out of joint with most people's understanding of religion which is normally associated with the supernatural.

These two objections, both seriously and strongly held, are going beyond the point and imputing significance which is not intended. An important element in the appeal of religions is that they do offer a view of the world which is both coherent and comprehensive. This does not mean that they explain everything — the place of suffering is a serious difficulty within the Christian faith — but they do offer a general view. Just as young children will work hard at making sense of their experiences of the physical environment (stone is hard, wool is soft) so most mature humans will try to make sense of the variety of their experiences both emotionally and physically.

Now this desire to make sense of things may result in different outcomes. Some may find that they can see no coherence, others may lose interest, others may find it in submission to one of the world's religions, others in Humanism and so on. This does not make Humanism and Marxism religions, it means rather that they have things in common with religions. This is why they have often been called 'quasi-religions' or, to use more modern jargon, 'non-religious stances for living'.

The most important point emerging from this section is that the desire to make sense of these fundamental life questions is an important source of *motivation* in the religious quest and therefore something for teachers to develop and to extend. To do so is to engage the students in a process without prescribing the outcome. Clearly the teenage years are the ones when these questions are most agonised over but younger children do ask these questions in different guises which teachers would do well to listen to carefully and to encourage.

Religion, therefore, is likely to begin with a search for meaning though not all outcomes will be necessarily religious. This brings us back again to the question at the beginning of the chapter, 'what is religion?'

Religion as a Six-dimensional Activity

It was noted early in the chapter how difficult it is to define religion. An alternative approach is to try to describe it. There is a considerable

What Do We Mean By Religion?

amount of activity going on in the world which is commonly described as being religious. Countless millions claim to belong to one religion or another and most of the globe is covered with places of worship and religious devotion. To look at the practice of religions in the world might be a much more fruitful way of looking at the breadth of religion. This was the approach adopted by Ninian Smart[1] and the result of his analysis of his observation of religion was summarized in his six dimensions.

There is nothing sacrosanct about Smart's account, others might well do it differently. It is discussed in detail here because many have found it a very helpful tool in understanding religion and it has also been used as a basis for certain approaches to religious education.

Smart's six dimensions of religion are:

(i) doctrinal;
(ii) mythological;
(iii) ethical;
(iv) ritual;
(v) experiential;
(vi) social.

These could also be seen as the different facets of a jewel. Each one can be studied separately but they are all facets of the one gem and as such are interrelated and interconnected indissolubly.

Doctrinal Dimensions

Every religion has at its centre a set of doctrines or beliefs which form part of its foundation. These doctrines, which would be about a religious vision of ultimate reality, may be elaborately worked out in philosophical terms as they are in some religions or they may be expressed in vague and less coherent ways. In Christianity, the central doctrines are expressed in the official creeds of the church, notably the Nicene Creed, and focus upon the two basic doctrines: the Trinity (God in three persons, Father, Son and Holy Spirit) and the Incarnation (the entry of God the Son into humanity in the person of Jesus Christ). Within Judaism there is great stress upon the oneness of God and his loving kindness. In Hinduism there is a central belief in Brahman, the life force, and in the millions of gods who manifest the 'One'. Within Islam there is a strict emphasis upon Unity and upon the uniqueness of God. These doctrines are binding upon the believer. Five times each day the Muslim confesses 'There is no God but Allah and Mohammed is his prophet'. In Baptism, the Christian rite of initiation, the follower confesses belief in the divine Trinity. There will inevitably be different levels of understanding of the doctrinal systems between, say, educated and simple followers and there will be different interpretations of the doctrines, some being more literal or more symbolic than others. Nevertheless, doctrines are a crucial dimension of any religion and are an analysis and codification of what is expressed in the mythological dimension.

Mythological Dimension

The mythological dimension, often called the *story* dimension, is the means of conveying the teaching of a religion through stories, poems, legends, hymns and so on. Mythological can be an unhelpful term, developing as it does from the noun 'myth' which in common understanding has come to mean an untrue tale. However, in its more technical sense it derives from the Greek 'muthos' which means literally 'story'. To describe the sacred stories of the world's religions as mythological is therefore no comment upon their historical truth. The term is quite neutral.

Within 'stories' would certainly be included the accounts of the lives of the founders: the stories of Moses, of the Lord Buddha, of Mohammed, of the Ten Gurus, of Jesus. Within the Hindu tradition, there is a vast amount of material from the Vedas. The significance of the mythological dimension is that it is another vehicle for expressing the teaching of a religion. For Christians, for example, an essential part of the year is the keeping of Holy Week and Easter. From Palm Sunday, through the week to Maundy Thursday, Good Friday, Holy Saturday and finally to Easter Day, the believers go through in mind Jesus' entry into Jerusalem, his teaching in the Temple, his last supper with his disciples, his betrayal in the Garden of Gethsemane, his arrest, trial, crucifixion, death, burial and finally his Resurrection. This is done lovingly each year because in these stories is laid out the central mystery of the Christian faith, the reconciliation of God and humanity. Whether or not these stories have attached to them legendary accretions is not of first significance — what matters is that they both express and also feed the experience of believers.

Often there is dispute among believers in a particular tradition about the historical status of a story or series of stories. A case in point are the Nativity stories in the Gospels, with especially reference to the virginal conception of Jesus. The stories are about the entry of 'God-made-man' into human affairs and hence are of great significance for believers. For very many believers these stories are an historical account of what actually happened This was the way that God chose for Jesus to enter humanity. Others would say that the story of the virginal conception is an example of a symbolic story or a myth — a story written to convey the understanding that here was someone entering the world who was quite different from anybody who had done so before. In one sense both groups of believers are expressing the same conviction though they generally do not approve of each other's approach!

Ethical Dimension

All religions lay upon their followers a way of life which ought to be followed. Judaism, for example, has always placed great importance upon the Torah, the revealed law of God. When a Jewish boy reaches adolescence he has his Barmitzvah, his coming of age, when he becomes (literally) a son of the law. This means that he takes upon himself the responsibility of the law. The Torah centres upon the Ten Commandments which are binding upon all Jews. Islam, in the Koran, also lays down detailed requirements of Muslims which include even styles of dress. An important requirement is one of hospitality. Within Christianity the law of charity (or love) — loving God, and your neighbour as yourself — is supreme and Christians are pointed to the life of Jesus as an example for living.

Most religions have an important place for 'saints', people within the tradition who by their life and works have given an example to others and are often described as 'lights'. The study of such people has played an important part in much religious teaching and still has a special place today.

In the modern world religions are increasingly being challenged to develop and express ethical attitudes towards such matters as nuclear weapons and ecology. In some senses this is not a new problem as all living religious traditions have the constant task of applying their ethical principles to the issues of the day.

Ritual Dimension

The ritual dimension encompasses all those actions and activities which worshippers *do* in the practice of their religion. It ranges from the closing of eyes in prayer to participation on a once-in-a-lifetime pilgrimage. It includes services, festivals, ceremonies, customs, traditions, clothing, symbols. In many ways the ritual dimension is the shop window of a religion. The following would come within the limits of the ritual dimension: Muslims removing their shoes outside the mosque, Sikhs and Jews covering their heads before worship, Sikhs wearing the five symbols of their faith (the five Ks), Christians being present at a celebration of the eucharist, the celebration of the coming of age in the Barmitzvah, the making of pilgrimage to holy places whether it be Jerusalem, Mecca or Amritsah, the celebration of festivals: Diwali, Christmas, Passover, Guru Nanak's birthday and so on.

The ritual dimension is very closely associated with the stories of a religion. Very often they are enactments of the stories. In Judaism an historical event of great significance is the rescuing of the people from Egypt in the Exodus. This is very deep within Jewish feeling. The Passover meal, celebrated annually in the home, is a re-enactment of the original meal and in the course of the meal the ancient story is recounted. The Christian eucharist is a re-enactment of Christ's death and resurrection and is seen as making it real in the present.

There is a danger in talking of ritual of serious misunderstanding. In much common language words like ritual and ritualistic are used in a pejorative sense. Ritual is seen as something which is empty or fussy or formal, something which is devoid of any real meaning or significance. Certainly anything can degenerate into this state but in this context ritual is merely a descriptive term of the activities in a religion which are significant to its followers. Rituals provide the framework for both the sustaining and deepening of the worshipper's faith. They reflect too the devotion of worshippers — look at the faces of pilgrims on the Haj or at Lourdes — and also often enhances that devotion ('I felt uplifted . . .').

The ritual dimension is much more akin to religious *feelings* than to religious doctrine. Of course the rituals reflect the doctrines but they really work upon the emotions of believers — and also upon others too. I remember being present with a small group of Western tourists of differing religious views amongst the vast crowds of worshippers in the Russian Orthodox Cathedral of Smolensk. The sound of the choir, the smell of the incense, the visual beauty of the building, the devotion of the congregation were all intensely moving and all the members of the group felt to some degree that, to quote the Orthodox themselves, they were in heaven.

Experiential Dimension

At the core of religion is feeling and the experiential dimension bears witness to this. Most, if not all, believers would claim that at the centre of their religion is an experience to some degree or other of the divine. In some individuals it comes in dramatic forms. In the Old Testament, Isaiah's searing vision in the Temple would certainly come in the first rank as would, of course, the visions of Mohammed. The experience of most believers are not in this league. For most the experience of the divine would be much less dramatic, though not less significant: a feeling of being in tune with creation, a feeling of being given strength in times of difficulty, a feeling, as John Wesley put it, of the heart at times being strangely warmed. This dimension is so important because it is this one which provides the motivation for the others and makes the practice of religion worthwhile. It is this experience, this feeling, which makes, for example, the performing of rituals a living and significant activity rather than a participation in an historical curiosity. The experiential dimension is closely related to the ritual dimensions in that it provides the incentive to participation but the festivals, pilgrimages and ceremonies also in turn feed, enrich and enhance the experience of believers. Pilgrims (as opposed to tourists) to Lourdes make the journey with some degree of expectation, visit the holy domaine there, are present at mass in the grotto, join in the Procession of the Blessed Sacrament, mingle with the sick and, on their return home would normally go with their commitment deepened and their spirits 'uplifted'. Their religious feelings motivate them to partake in the pilgrimage and the doing of it deepens those same feelings.

One of the problems about the experiential dimensions is that it is very difficult to describe religious experience in words. Naturally any attempt to do so must rely heavily upon such devices as symbolism, simile, metaphor and analogy. Isaiah's vision in the Temple and Moses and the Burning Bush are both well known Biblical examples of this. The problem is compounded where the religious education of younger children is concerned because on the one hand it is very important that children should develop some notion of religious *feeling* but on the other there is concern that the symbolism of many of the well known stories may be a barrier to this being achieved. There can be no doubt that young children do experience, in other than 'religious' contexts, the sort of emotions which are important in religious feeling — awe, wonder, an awareness of mystery, a sense of belonging and so on. These feelings should be fostered and this can be done in a number of ways which will be considered in the chapter on 'themes'. The debate still rages without resolution as to whether younger children should be told the stories like Moses and the Burning Bush so that they can perceive something of the 'feeling' upon which stories centre or whether the misconceptions which the children can pick up really make it more appropriate for the stories to be introduced to the children when they are older. It is perhaps a decision for each teacher to make.

Social Dimension

The social dimension of religion is concerned with the expression of that religion in society. Clearly it is closely related to the ethical dimension which gives guidance on how the faithful should live in the world. The social dimension is more concerned with the corporate nature of religious institutions. For example, in Judaism it is important to look closely at the organization of the synogogue and its relationship to the home. In Christianity, the church is obviously of central importance and within that the role of the bishop in the unity of the church and of the priest in the work of the individual parishes. Religious communities with the monks and nuns who constitute them are highly significant in most religions. All the time here one is stepping over into the ritual dimension but this is only to be expected as they are constantly interrelated and intertwined.

Two Implications for Teaching Children aged 5 to 12 years

Within this are two major implications for teachers which will be considered in greater detail later in the book.

1. Religion is partly a personal search for meaning which most children (and adults too!) even quite young ones, engage in. While it is much easier for older children whose thinking is in the formal operational stage to identify issues and to formulate their questions, younger children are just as interested in making sense of themselves, discovering who they are and attempting to grapple with many of the mysteries which surround them. Often though their questions and comments need

rather more unravelling by a teacher or parent than do the questions of older children. The adult needs to listen carefully, to ask questions (if appropriate) carefully and to help, in a very sensitive way, children to continue and progress in their search for meaning. The teacher's role is not to give answers because there are no answers which are universally agreed. It is rather to help the children to move along in the process of finding their own meaning.

2 The six dimensions of religion covering as they do such a vast and complex activity as a religion naturally include aspects which are highly cerebral and intellectually sophisticated and others which are essentially emotional and visual. From what we know of the development of children's religious understanding, some dimensions are clearly more suitable for younger children than others. Most teachers who have worked in this area and with children in the age range 5 to 12 years would pinpoint the most appropriate dimensions as:

social
ritual
mythological

To this list may be added some aspects of the experiential dimension though there are problems about this which are referred to earlier in this section. The ritual and the social dimensions are appropriate for younger children mainly because they are concrete and visual. The mythological dimension appeals to children's love of stories. The two dimensions, the doctrinal and the ethical, which have been omitted are both difficult for younger children.

The doctrinal is essentially intellectual and tends to raise questions which children of this age tend not to ask. Ten-year-old children are, on the whole, not very much interested in asking questions about the relationship between the divine and the human in the incarnate Jesus (doctrinal dimension) though they usually love to hear the Christmas stories (mythological dimension) and are often quite interested in learning about the Christmas ceremonies (ritual dimension). The ethical dimension can be difficult with younger children because it is not until they move into what Piaget calls the heteronomous stage that they are able to reflect about, rather than just accept, rules and this tends not to happen until the end of this age range.

Most religious material selected for study by children in the age range 5–12 years will therefore be drawn from the ritual, social and mythological dimensions of religion.

Note

1 Smart, N. (1968) *Secular Education and the Logic of Religion*, Faber.

5 An Implicit Approach Through Themes

In the past few years an approach to the teaching of religious education with younger children through the use of themes has become widespread. This was brought into prominence by Ronald Goldman under the name of *'life'* themes in 1965 and in 1973 reoriented by Michael Grimmitt under the title of *'depth'* themes.

The popularity of themes in the religious education of younger children arises out of the children's widely acknowledged problems in understanding many religious concepts. Goldman, as we have seen, described children up to the mental age of seven as being in a 'pre-religious' stage. This does not mean, of course, that children at this stage cannot respond to religion at an emotional level but that most religious concepts are beyond their understanding and their experience. Just as in the process of learning to read children go through various pre-reading activities, so, it is argued, in religious education, children need pre-religious education activities. The theme is intended to be just such a thing. The aim is, to use a horticultural metaphor, to provide a rich soil which will enable religious ideas and concepts presented in later years to flourish!

Life Themes and Depth Themes

So what then is a 'life' theme? Goldman made four points about them.

(i) They must start from the firsthand experience of children.
(ii) They should be about matters in which children are naturally interested.
(iii) They should relate religion to life.
(iv) Material from the Bible or any other explicit religious

material should not be brought in for its own sake but only where it can illuminate the children's understanding.

Two examples of life themes offered by Goldman are 'The Importance of Bread' and 'Homes'. The former starts with bread, an important religious metaphor (for example, 'I am the bread of life' [John, Chapter 6, verse 35]) as something within the first-hand experience of children, as something eaten, toasted and so on. The theme develops along lines in which most children are interested such as making bread and looking at the effects of yeast. It relates religion and life by placing real life experiences of bread and its significance for sustaining life alongside religious imagery and so illuminating children's understanding of the image. In this theme, too, one of the work cards looks specifically at bread making in the time of Jesus.

The second example 'Homes' covers areas such as: our own homes, homes in other lands (with a strong concentration on the home of Jesus) and families on the move. As with 'Bread', this 'life' theme starts from the first-hand experience of children and it continues in a variety of ways which interest most children. Its religious value, it is claimed, lies not primarily in the study of Jesus' home life but in the way that children will explore the home as a centre of love and mutual help and support. The section on families on the move, by raising and discussing children's mixed experiences of moving house and area, should lead to a greater understanding of the situation of the homeless. As religious education, this 'life' theme aims at enriching children's understanding and sympathy.

'Depth' themes as described by Michael Grimmitt are in many respects like 'life' themes. They both arise out of first-hand experience, they both follow natural interests, they both draw in subject matter from different areas and they both seek to provide the conditions for children's religious understanding to grow through a deepening awareness of their own ordinary experience.

Where the two approaches differ arises over the basic aim and intention. The Goldmanian 'life' theme seems to have two principal underlying aims: firstly, to foster insight in children using educationally more appropriate ways with the intention that it should lead to Christian commitment (or as one practitioner of the 'new' RE when it was new in the mid-1960s described it, 'an old flame tarted up!') and secondly, more specifically, to lead children into an understanding and appreciation of traditional Christian statements and images. This is evidenced by the inclusion of much Biblical material even when the connection is artificial. Goldman himself always claimed that it did not

An Implicit Approach Through Themes

matter if there was explicit religious material included in life themes or not, but his followers seemed to feel much happier if there was! The approach through 'depth' themes is more open. There would be a strong tendency *not* to include Biblical material and the hope would be that insight fostered through reflection upon personal experience would illuminate the understanding of *religion* rather than of Christianity in particular. The invitation is:

> Look more deeply into this familiar thing; do you see anything about it which you haven't seen before?

But Are Themes Religious?

Thematic teaching has been misunderstood by many teachers. Some have seen themes as convenient branches upon which to hang religion. One teacher went to enormous lengths to talk about homes, making a frieze of everybody's house in the class, acting out scenes from the home and then switching to Jesus' home at Nazareth. All that went before was seen as an introduction to the real 'religious education' and its major function was to excite as much interest as possible. Other teachers have rejected themes because they do not see them in any way as 'religious'. Take a theme like 'Friends', it may be exciting, lead to lots of drama, art work, stories, but how is it 'religious'? Some have even suggested that thematic teaching is a plot to 'water down' religious education.

Both these groups share an underlying assumption about religious education, that it is about passing on to children certain facts and stories to do with religion — life in Palestine at the time of Jesus, certain stories about Jesus or about Mohammed and so on. It is these stories which are seen as the religious content. This view is very understandable. Very many teachers are concerned that the children they teach should not grow up religiously illiterate and giving them some content like this would prevent that happening. However, it does reveal a fundamental misunderstanding of what thematic teaching is trying to do.

As we have seen themes are designed to help children, at their own level, to explore human experience and relationships and this for two reasons.

   1   As we have seen already, religion is concerned with asking and offering answers to certain questions which most, if not all,

people ask themselves at some time or other, questions such as 'who am I?' 'Is there purpose in living?' 'Is death the end?' 'What sense is there in evil and suffering?'. These 'frontier' questions, as they are often called, underlie religious systems. It is often claimed that people turn to religions at times of crisis and hardship and it may be partly because crises and hard times raise these questions more forcibly. Few young children are going to be asking questions articulated with such sophistication but they do ask similar questions at their own level. Investigating such themes as 'Who am I?', or 'Friends' or 'Hands' will help them to develop some sense of self-hood and of relationships, good and bad, which they experience. Their concerns will be a long way from those of Plato but the difference will be one of degree rather than one of kind!

2 Much religious language and symbolism is inevitably second-hand. It is notoriously difficult to convey deeply felt emotion or experience in words yet sometimes this must be done. The normal method is to convey it through simile or metaphor. Religions, when they want to convey meaning, tend to draw metaphors from human experience. Hence, prevalent images are of the family or of the lover and the beloved. Illustrating this from Christian language, there is the pervading image of the family: God as father, Jesus as son, the church as the family of God, members of the human race as the children of God, people as brothers and sisters. Such imagery, in one sense so potent, can also become dry, formal and tired. By encouraging children to reflect upon 'Homes and Families' or 'Friends' or 'Hands' or 'Children around the World', we are providing them with opportunities to enrich their own understanding and experience so that when they meet the imagery it is illuminated by their own experience.

The principal difference between the supporters of thematic teaching and those who are not seems to hinge around the definition of religion. To the former group, the *whole* of the theme is religious education (to use the technical term, it is *implicit* religious education), to the latter group the religious part is that which has an explicitly identified religious content. This, on the whole, is an unproductive dispute. It can certainly be argued that if religious teaching was specifically excluded from schools tomorrow, teachers of young children would still go on doing themes on 'Homes' and so on. This does not, of course, mean that such themes are not religious it merely means that

An Implicit Approach Through Themes

they are not *exclusively* religious. It seems best to stick to our earlier term of 'pre-religious'; that thematic work is a basis for an understanding of religion.

Two examples, taken from the accounts of two teachers, one an experienced class teacher, the other a student teacher, illustrate this.

This first one, from the experienced teacher, who described herself as 'not conventionally religious' records a moment of discovery from observing a child:

> One of the religious stories which has always had the most meaning for me is the story of Moses and the Burning Bush in the Old Testament. Ever since I was a child I have been rivetted by it. I can picture vividly the blue sky, the bare rock, the hot sun, the sparse vegetation. I can sense the silence and the aloneness of Moses. I can imagine his mounting surprise at the bush burning and not being consumed and the slow and fearful realisation that he was in the presence of Majesty. I think that a sense of awe and wonder is lacking in many children's experience and so each year I have told my 6-year-olds this story. I know that it is quite a difficult story but I told it simply and with lots of expression and drama. I know too that I told it well because the children were always spellbound but I always sensed that it did not speak to them in the way that it did to me. Recently I had a final year student on teaching practice in my class and I was banished to a tiny room with the four children in most need of extra teaching and attention. I did many things with the four and got to know them very well. One thing we did was to plant seeds and I shall never forget the shout of joy from one little boy when he suddenly noticed the first shoot penetrating the soil, nor the look on his face. There was excitement, and joy — and wonder. His feeling then was what I had tried unsuccessfully to foster in my Moses and the Burning Bush.

This account speaks for itself: the only way for children, or adults for that matter, to understand the story of Moses and the Burning Bush (as opposed to just knowing what happened in it) is for them to have had some experience of awe, wonder and mystery already. It may come through a sprouting seed, or seeing a new-born baby, a litter of newly-born rabbits or the night sky for the first time. Only with some degree of prior experience of this kind can the hearer see deeply into the story of Moses and then experience enlightens experience.

Religious Education 5–12

The second example comes from a student's account of some of her teaching in a church school with 7-year-olds.

> There had been so much fighting and squabbling in the playground over the week that the headmistress said that we really ought to get to grips with it. This is a church school and we ought to be teaching them to love their neighbours.
>
> After dinner I sat all the children down on the carpet and began to tell them about Jesus and loving their neighbours as themselves. I succeeded in getting them to talk about the terrible things that had happened in the playground — who had called who what and who had done what to whom. They were all very good and they all agreed that you shouldn't be unkind to other people but I had a feeling that I didn't get very far. It seemed when I thought about it that it's a very difficult idea to understand quite apart from putting it into practice. Perhaps it can only be done by seeing other people doing it. The more I thought about it the more it seemed that they have to have some idea of who their neighbour is and what loving or having concern means and that they would have to *feel* it as well.

The student's inexperience in teaching is clearly evidenced here but she has learned the valuable lesson that it is no good telling children things and expecting them to understand them if they have not had the relevant experience!

To summarize so far:

Thematic teaching as a basis for religious education:

(i) starts from the first hand experience of children;
(ii) is concerned with matters in which children are naturally interested.

It aims to provide children with the opportunity:

(i) to examine and see more deeply into their own experiences and feelings;
(ii) to become more aware of the experience and feelings of other people;
(iii) to see themselves in relationship with other people.

Example Number 1

Hands

Hands has been a popular theme topic over a number of years, mainly because it seems to many teachers to be especially appropriate for younger children. It certainly fulfils the condition of arising out of the immediate experience of children: hands, after all, are a major tool in coping with the world and life. For this reason too it will fulfil the second condition of dealing with matters in which children are naturally interested. 'Hands' should therefore also provide an opportunity for children to explore their normal experience more deeply.

This is how one teacher developed it with 7-year-old children, allowing three hours per week for seven weeks.

Aims to help children:

(i) to investigate the importance of hands in daily living;
(ii) to consider ways in which hands can be used with regard to other people;
(iii) to begin to be aware of the interrelatedness of human society.

Development

(i) Discussion on the importance of hands. Things we need our hands for. Trying to do things without using hands. Children without hands.
(ii) Different ways that people use their hands towards others
    (a) Hands that *help*.
    (b) Hands that *heal*.
    (c) Hands that *work*.
    (d) Hands that *hurt*.
    (e) Hands that *create*.
    (f) *Empty* hands.

This latter list arose out of discussion with the children together with a degree of codification from the teacher. In each case, the work arose from the children's first-hand experience and moved to look at examples on a broader scale.

For example, hands that heal began naturally from the children's experience of being bandaged up after falls while playing. Most had hospital experiences either as a patient or as a visitor and could talk and write about this. A nurse came into school to talk to the children about the sort of work she did in the hospital. The children also raised Florence Nightingale and Mother Teresa of Calcutta, both of whose work had recently been featured on television programmes. Some children did some fact finding about them from reference books and a few organized a collection of money for Mother Teresa's work.

Hands that hurt, which perhaps had the function of preventing the theme from slipping into sentimentality, began with a discussion of unpleasant happenings in the school playground and developed into an (amazingly) informed discussion of crime, theft, murder, urban terrorism and so on which the children had gleaned from television news programmes.

The work reached its climax in a school assembly when the class displayed it and talked about it to the whole school. It was brought together in the song 'He's got the whole world in his hands' to which the children added their own additional verses. 'He's got Mother Teresa in his hands', 'He's got the birds and the butterflies in his hands'. For a backcloth the children made a huge circle to represent the world and on this they stuck examples of their work.

In the teacher's view the theme went well. In an extract from his evaluation he writes:

> In general terms the children enjoyed the theme and so worked at it with reasonable enthusiasm. It stimulated a lot of written work which in general was well above average for the class. It fostered a considerable amount of oral language work and set quite a few children off on the task of finding information out from books. As far as the more specific aims were concerned I have no doubt that it did have the effect of making children more aware of the importance of helpfulness, compassion and a caring attitude. I won't claim that it worked miracles in terms of actual behaviour but it did certainly widen the children's horizons.

Now some will argue that this theme on 'Hands', admirable though it might be, is not really religious education. Rather it could be described as 'values' education or moral education. It is merely attempting to initiate children into what is basically a generally agreed way of approaching living — 'a low level moral consensus' as it has been called. If religious education were to be removed from the curriculum, it is argued, this sort of theme would still happen. Some teachers have in fact added a fourth aim to the theme, namely 'to present Jesus as the model' and therefore to tell some of the stories of Jesus helping and healing and so on as examples of the use of hands.

An Implicit Approach Through Themes

Two comments can be made in response to this. Firstly, that to add such an aim, while entirely appropriate in a church school or Sunday school, may be less so in schools which have no specific religious basis and may be less attractive to teachers who do not themselves see Jesus in such a way.

Secondly, the 'religious' nature of the theme can be seen not in the explicit stories it includes of religious figures but in the development of certain attitudes and ways of looking at the world and at other people. The underlying aims of this theme on 'Hands' are those which are central to all the major religions of the world. They are also important to very many people who would not wish to identify themselves with any one religion. The theme is therefore not *exclusively* religious but this does not make it any the less an important step in the development of religious understanding.

Example Number 2

Homes and Families

Homes and families is also a very popular theme in primary schools.

Aims

To help children:
- (i) to look more closely at the families in which they live;
- (ii) to gain insights into a wide range of concepts such as love, security, consideration, sharing;
- (iii) to begin to see what it means to belong to a wider community;
- (iv) (for older children) to gain some pictures of how families from other cultures live;
- (v) to begin to perceive the application of the metaphor of the family.

It is possible to use this theme at any stage from 5 to 12 years though, of course, both the concepts and the content would be different. Threads too would run through it: the house, the home, family, extended family, pets, neighbours, family celebrations, different patterns both historical and contemporary of family life, animals and their families, wider families — the school, the world and so on. (All teachers recognize the need for caution and sensitivity in talking about this area.)

With very young children a teacher might attempt to talk about and paint pictures of our homes:

> to identify who makes up the family;
> to talk about being looked after;
> to talk about looking after pets;
> to discuss family celebrations, birthdays, anniversaries, Christmas, christenings, weddings;
> to introduce (perhaps) children around the world.

Throughout, the detailed selection and treatment of the content would be controlled by the aims, at a level appropriate to the age and stage of the children.

With 7–9-year-old children the children might focus upon 'raising a family'.

— talk about how mammals and birds raise their young
— making the home (nest, drey, etc)
— of what materials, how is it built? Why is it designed in that way?
— how are the young cared for after they are born?
— how are they protected?
— how are they fed, kept warm?
— what sort of skills do the parent animals teach the young?
— what is the relationship of parents and offspring after the latter are grown?
— talk about human families and how children are raised
— pursue the same questions asked about birds and mammals to draw out the similarities and differences.

With 10–12-year-old children, the teacher might begin to focus upon looking at homes and family patterns which are different to those of the children themselves. This could be done by looking at families in different countries or, perhaps, families from different cultures who are living in their midst.

For example, it might be useful to look at patterns of family life of a Muslim family whose origin is in the Indian sub-continent. Work could cover the relationship of family life to Islam, family festivals, the mosque and such notions as extended family, authority and arranged marriages. (*NB* this would involve studying a considerable amount of explicit religious material but this would be secondary and not the principal point of the theme in a religious education scheme.)

An Implicit Approach Through Themes

Another approach could be to consider wider communities — the school, the church, the human race — as families and so to explore the implications of this metaphor.

NB A number of teachers would wish to add to the content of this theme some work on the home of Jesus. It would be argued that this would be a natural way of introducing background material to the life and teaching of Jesus. This is, of course, perfectly acceptable providing:

(a) that it is a natural development and not dragged in; and
(b) that this section is not seen as the part which gives the theme its authenticity as a piece of religious education.

Example Number 3

People

Aims

To help children:

(i) to begin to see that they belong to a wider community (a 'big family');
(ii) to begin to see that most people both need and are able to give help;
(iii) to begin to be aware of the interrelatedness of human society;
(iv) to begin to identify specific examples of help.

This can be used at different stages but is probably most popular with younger children.

Possible development

Talk about friends — what makes a friend?

People who are friends to us: family — parents, grandparents, aunts, brothers and sisters, neighbours.

People who are *like* friends to us — nurses, firemen, policemen — ways in which they serve us.

Specific groups in the community who need special consideration. For example, the old — ways in which we can help them — shopping, weeding, etc.

— ways in which they can help us — with their

experience of life and the time they have to listen.

(If done with 8 year olds and above). International help — the work of Oxfam and Christian Aid. The contribution of overseas workers to our social services.

Teachers will, of course, follow such a theme in different ways according to individual interests and available resources. Some will concentrate very heavily upon the section 'People who are *like* friends to us', perhaps looking at a variety of categories here, so that it becomes 'People who help us'. There will be varying opportunities in different areas for children to make visits to fire station or Police station or to receive firemen or policemen into the school. Local factors will also to a large extent determine whether children can be involved in some practical helping. It is envisaged that using such a theme would involve work in poetry, drama and dance as well as in the more usual talking, writing and art activities.

Example Number 4

Joy and Happiness (for very young children)

Aims

To help children to:

(i) reflect upon what they enjoy doing;
(ii) examine the variety of ways in which this emotion occurs by looking at the senses.

Possible Development

Things I see — things I love seeing — colours, toys, parents, woods, television — things I would miss if I could not see.

Things I touch — the delight in feeling — smooth, rough, hard, soft, prickly, corrugated. Things I love to touch — holding a baby, soft toys or clothing, stroking a pet.

Things I can smell — different smells I can recognize (fresh bread, orange, cheese, chocolate, coffee, gravy powder, mint. Smells I love.

Things I hear — different sounds — the sea, animal noises, music, singing, laughter. Sounds I love best.

An Implicit Approach Through Themes

Additional Themes

Many themes can play their part in laying the foundations for religious understanding providing they fulfil the conditions laid down earlier, namely, to help children:

(i) to examine and see more deeply into their own experiences and feelings;
(ii) to become more aware of the experiences and feelings of others;
(iii) to see themselves in relationship with other people.

Some which have been found more suitable than many for this purpose include:

Friends	Birthdays
Neighbours	Caring
Gifts	Pets
Mothers and fathers	Colour
The seasons	Myself
Journeys	Food and hunger
Courage	Forgiveness

Developing Natural Incidents

It very often happens that situations arise unexpectedly in a class in which a teacher can see the possibilities for developing religious understanding. Much depends here upon the perception and skill of the teacher but much fruitful work can be done in this almost 'incidental' way.

Below is an example of how a gifted teacher picked up the mood of a group of children and developed it. The situation was the first day of a school camp. The children were from South London, many with little experience of the countryside and most below average in terms of educational achievement. In the diary of the week kept by one of the boys, full as it was of rushed, untidy and misspelt work this particular extract stood out. It has been tidied up.

> We cleared up our dinner. I had to wash up with Paul and Scott. Miss ... said that anybody who broke anything would have to pay for it. Marie and Karen helped Mr ... light the camp fire. We all sat round it on rugs. It was really lovely. It was warm and I liked watching the flames. We sang songs. The

fire died down and it got very dark. Mr ... said that it was time to get ready for bed. Then Gary shouted 'Look at the sky'. I looked up and got a funny feeling inside. It was so dark and there were millions and millions of stars. Some were very big, others were very tiny like pin pricks. Miss ... told us that it had taken millions of years for the light from some of those stars to reach us and that a lot of them were not there any more — they had got burnt out. I felt really tiny. I never felt like this before.

This was clearly this child's first deep experience of awe and wonder. Now set beside this the teacher's own account in her diary of what happened.

The most remarkable part of the day was the end of camp fire. The children had enjoyed a cosy session around the fire singing songs and telling jokes. At the end as the fire got very low we said 'Bedtime' Then suddenly Gary piped up 'Look at the sky' and everybody did! It *was* a remarkable sky, very dark and very clear, and the absense of lights around us enhanced its clarity. It was a whole mass of stars. Everyone was very silent for a few minutes and then someone said 'There's millions of them'. I explained very quietly about light years and how long it had taken the light to come from some of the stars. Of course it was a new experience for them and I think it awed them a bit.

The feeling of awe and wonder described haltingly but effectively in the child's extract is one which can only be known *through experiencing it*. No amount of talking will convey it yet it is an essential experience for 'getting inside' religion. This does not mean that an experience of the 'numinous' is necessarily religious. Many people who do not regard themselves as religious have had similar experiences but such experiences are nevertheless an integral part of the experience of religious people.

It is possible to work with children in certain ways which are more likely to evoke feelings of awe and wonder: growing things, thinking about rainbows, studying and handling crystals, things I love doing and so on, but it is still very difficult to succeed in evoking such feelings. Most teachers probably hope that they are around when children have these experiences so that they can either gently sustain them or, as in the extract above, enhance and develop them.

There will be many times in the year when a teacher can pick up

An Implicit Approach Through Themes

and develop natural incidents in the classroom and so assist the development of children's religious understanding — from caring, sharing, kindness and so on. Much effective religious education, certainly with younger children, happens in this way.

6 An Introduction to Five Religions

In recent years the content of the religious education syllabuses has broadened to include the study of aspects of a number of religions and this is now a staple ingredient in most religious education programmes. This development arises partly because of greater interest shown by society at large in different religions, particularly Eastern religions, and partly because there are now living in most western countries active adherents of a number of religions. In Britain, for example, there are significant groups of Hindus, Jews, Muslims and Sikhs. The problem posed for the teacher who is not a religious education specialist is one of knowledge.

This chapter attempts to look at five religions: Christianity, Hinduism, Judaism, Islam and Sikhism and to give an introduction to them emphasizing those aspects which are perhaps more suitable for the education of children aged 5–12 years. These five have been chosen because it is these which are most common in Britain. Buddhism has not been considered in this way because, although in world terms, it is an important and significant religion, it is much less likely to be in evidence in this society. These introductions are brief ones and as such they are intended only to provide a very basic framework of knowledge, enough to enable teachers to approach some of the books listed in chapter 17 with more confidence.

In the next chapter, there will be a consideration of some of the issues and the approaches to introducing children to religious material drawn from a range of traditions.

Christianity

Doctrines

Christianity, like Judaism and Islam, is based on the belief in one God but conceives him as a Trinity, three Persons, or aspects, within the Unity, the Father, the Son and the Holy Spirit. These aspects express the different spheres of God's activity: as creator, as redeemer and as life giver. Christianity believes that the most important characteristic of God's nature is love and this is worked out in its other cardinal doctrine, the Incarnation. Christianity is rooted in the belief that, out of love for the human race, God himself entered humanity and took flesh in the person of Jesus Christ. In the life, death and Resurrection of Jesus Christ, Christians believe that they have both seen the nature of God in terms which they can understand and that they have also been reconciled with, and accepted by, God. All those who followed Jesus and are baptised constitute the Church, often called the Body of Christ, in which the Holy Spirit dwells.

Jesus Christ

Absolutely central to the Christian faith is the person of Jesus Christ. Within Christian teaching, he is more than a teacher or a prophet. In the New Testament he is called by many titles; the most enduring have been 'Son of God' and 'Lord'. As one who is the personification of God's love, Christ fills a unique position as the Way, the Truth and the Life. Little really is known of the life of Jesus. Mark, the earliest gospel, begins with Jesus' appearance at John's Baptism. Matthew and Luke give accounts of his birth, though not all Christians would accept these as historical accounts. The four gospels do not purport to be biographies of Jesus, but rather as works with the aim of demonstrating who Jesus is. St John (chapter 20, verse 31) says 'but these are written that you might believe that Jesus is the Christ, the Son of God'. This helps to account for the selection of material in the Gospels. In Mark, for example, out of sixteen chapters, six are devoted to the final week in Jesus' life, which indicates the significance that Mark attached to these seven days.

Because Jesus is perceived by Christians as the revealer of God's nature, special attention is paid to the gospels as they contain his words and works. In the Eucharist, when the set passage from the Gospel is read, it is normal for the congregation to stand as a mark of recognition of its significance. As the mediator Christians address their prayers to God through him, and as Incarnate Lord, he is himself the object of worship.

The Bible

For all Christians the Bible is a very special book, though different traditions within Christianity disagree as to how exactly it is special. Some Christians see the Bible as the revelation of God — that through the words of scripture, the unseen God reveals his character and his ways to people. Other Christians are more inclined to see the Bible as a human record of mankind's experience of God in history. How the Bible is perceived will determine how it is used. Some search the Bible for detailed guidance on the living of daily life, others look for general principles. Some see the Bible as the only source of Christian belief, others will place alongside it the tradition and experience of the Church.

The Bible is a book of faith, telling as it does, the history of the Jewish people and seeing in it the activity of God. It is interpreted history. The New Testament is the same. In the accounts of Jesus and in the history of the very early church, the hand of God is seen. It is within this overall context that many of the famous stories of Christianity (and of Judaism too) are found: the Creation stories, the heroes (like Moses, Joshua and Samson) the prophets (like Amos, Isaiah and Jeremiah) the Kings, the Exodus from Egypt, the coming of Christ, his ministry, his death and resurrection, the whole story of the early Christian leaders such as Peter and Paul. The stories, of course, do not finish with the end of the New Testament. The 2000 years of subsequent history have produced many supremely significant events and people, right up to the present time.

Closely tied up with the sacred stories of Christianity are festivals and worship.

Festivals

As in all religions, festivals are highly important in the Christian round. The two principal festivals, Easter and Christmas, arise out of central events in the life of Christ. Others arise out of other events in His life and from the lives of saints. A much fuller account of Christian festivals is found elsewhere in this book.

Worship

Formal worship has always played a very important part in Christianity. For most Christians the principal service is that which is called the eucharist, holy communion, Lord's supper, holy mysteries or mass. For some, like the Quakers or the Salvation Army, the holy communion is never celebrated and for some other groups such as the Baptists it is celebrated less frequently than weekly. Throughout Christendom for the large majority, though, the eucharist is the centre of worship. Whatever form it takes — and it can vary from a simple said service to an elaborate sung celebration — the central action of eucharist is the taking of bread and wine and blessing them. This derives directly from the account of Jesus' last supper with his disciples when he blessed bread and wine and distributed them. In the eucharist the words of Christ are used and it is believed that in some sense the bread becomes the Body of Christ and the wine the Blood of Christ which worshippers then receive. The eucharist brings to mind the life, death and resurrection of Christ and while a small number of Christians would see it simply as a memorial, most Christians would be more inclined to see the eucharist as a making effective in the present the life giving sacrifice of Christ.

Baptism

The rite of entry or initiation into the Christian Church is Baptism. Although this can be administered at any age, and certain Christian groups like Baptists will only permit adults to be baptised, most baptisms are of infants. Baptism requires a decision on the part of the one being baptised to turn away from evil and to follow Christ. In the case of infants or young children this decision is taken on their behalf by godparents or sponsors who promise to see that they are brought up in Christian ways. In Baptism water is central to the rite: the persons being baptised are immersed in water or (more usually) sprinkled three times, in the names of the Father, the Son and the Holy Spirit, and signed on the forehead with a cross. Often a candle is lit to signify that they have passed from darkness to light. Names given in Baptism become Christian names; hence (the popular term 'Christening').

Religious Education 5–12

Confirmation

In Western Christendom, in the traditional churches, confirmation is the time when people baptised as infants can take upon themselves the promises made on their behalf by their godparents. This often happens in adolescence though it can happen at any age beyond that. In the traditional churches candidates for confirmation are brought to the bishop who lays his hands upon them. The candidates are asked the same questions as their godparents were at their baptism and now they take the promises upon themselves. In the Eastern Orthodox Churches babies are baptised and confirmed at the same time.

Marriage

Within the Christian religion, marriage is intended as a lifelong union between a man and a woman, entered into freely. Only one spouse is allowed at any one time and whereas widows and widowers can contract another marriage, the traditional churches do not remarry those who have been divorced. Weddings normally take place in church, though in the United States of America they may be performed in a variety of other places, such as a house or a garden. Marriage services centre around the making of vows to love, cherish and honour and the receiving of the blessing of God, mediated by the priest or minister.

Marriage customs vary though it is traditional for the bride to wear a white gown. In the United States bridegrooms normally wear white as well, though in Europe, dark clothing is more normal.

Marriages, because they signify a new life for the couple involved, are naturally occasions for rejoicing. They are usually, though not necessarily, accompanied by receptions, by dances, by the giving of gifts for the new home.

Death

Christian funerals are a mixture of rejoicing that the deceased is going to be with God and sadness at the parting and the separation. A traditional funeral would involve the funeral office said in church, perhaps with a requiem mass, followed by the committal of the body to the ground or to burning. Very often now the funeral service takes place at the chapel of the crematorium, or in the USA, in the funeral home.

Ethics

Christianity has always laid stress upon the importance of this world and of living properly within it. In its infancy, Christianity was often called the Way because it was seen as a way of life which stemmed from both the teaching of Jesus and from its worship. When pressed by questions, Jesus himself never pointed to an ethical code but rather to an ethical principle: 'love God' and 'love your neighbour as yourself' were the twin pivots of his moral teaching. This notion of loving too was seen more in doing rather than in emotional feeling. Loving could be seen as doing to others as you would like them to do unto you. This is reaffirmed in the early Christian literature and to it is added the notion of following the examples of Christ, as he is described in the Gospels.

Ethical feeling tends to go beyond the bounds of personal morality of one individual to another. For example there is great concern for the underprivileged, the dispossessed, the hungry and the suffering and there is considerable active work for justice and peace. There is a deep Christian conviction that in serving the poor and needy Christ himself is being served. A mark of Christian missionaries in the nineteenth century, for example — and they are certainly not exempt from criticism at the present time — was the building of hospitals and schools where these did not exist before. There is a growing feeling among Christians too for ecology which arises from the belief that mankind is the custodian of the created order.

The Social Dimension

The chief social phenomenon created by Christianity is the church. The church is variously described but it is seen primarily as the Body of Christ in the world or as the community of believers. Sometimes the term church is used of the local congregation or gathering, sometimes it is used in a national or international sense. Within the church there are a number of denominations and sects. Each one tends to have its own traditions and emphases.

It is possible to distinguish four main divisions in Christendom:

(i) the traditional churches, for example, the Roman Catholic, the Orthodox and the Anglican;
(ii) the mainstream protestant churches, for example, the Presbyterian, the Baptist and the Methodist;

(iii) the newer protestant churches such as the Pentecostals and the Seventh Day Adventists;
(iv) the fringe Christian sects such as the Jehovah's Witnesses and the Mormons.

During the twentieth century a marked feature of church life has been the ecumenical movement or the move towards church unity. A number of small churches have merged, though in the traditional churches, relationships are warm and cooperative, there have been no such moves as yet.

A particularly significant movement within the church has been, and is, monasticism. The idea behind monasticism is that men and women join together in religious communities or houses living a life under a rule. Each individual monk or nun after a period of noviceship makes vows of poverty, chastity and obedience. Monasteries have been and are powerful centres of prayer, of culture and of influence. Most monks and nuns are found in the traditional churches, though there is the famous ecumenical monastery at Taize in central France founded by Brother Roger, a member of the Reformed Church, which is so influential among young people.

Hinduism

To attempt in any way to describe Hinduism briefly is an almost impossible undertaking, especially for a Westerner. It has no recognized founder, no single sacred book and it resists attempts to codify it too closely. It is a religion of contrasts. It is broad, tolerant and inclusive. It has been described as the religion of Indians who are not members of another religion such as Sikhism, Buddhism or Christianity.

A central idea of Hinduism is what Westerners often call reincarnation or what the Hindu would call *samsara*, which we might interpret as transmigration or rebirth. Life is conceived of as a wheel, a wheel of birth, death, rebirth, a second death and so on, repeated over and over again. According to the merits of the present life, the soul is reborn into another form of life on earth. Good actions lead to rebirth into a higher form of life, bad actions to a lower form of life. This is often called the Law of Karma. A Hindu would therefore hope for a good Karma and so be reborn into a higher state.

The goal of life is to escape from this wheel of existence and so to be released from it (moksha). The soul can then be united with Brahman, the spirit which underlies all creation. This liberation from

An Introduction to Five Religions

the wheel of existence can be achieved in many different ways for example, through meditation, through performing the duties of one's daily life selflessly and through devotion (bhakti) to a particular god.

Brahman and the Gods

There is a strong impression in the West that Hindus worship many gods — perhaps hundreds and thousands of them! A traveller through India would pass many temples each with its own image of its god so it is not surprising that this view prevails. Most Hindus, though, would see all the deities as manifestations of the ONE, Brahman. The Rig Veda says: 'He is one but wise men call him by many names'. Brahman, the power underlying creation, is both the source and the sustainer of all things. Brahman is beyond description. The numerous gods are but windows to Brahman. Hindus do not worship the *images* of the gods in the temples but they worship that to which they point. They know perfectly well that they are made of clay or metal!

Although there are millions of manifestations of Brahman, there are three which stand above all:

Brahma — the creator of life
Vishnu — the preserver of life
Shiva — the destroyer of life

Vishnu, as the preserver of life, is thought to have taken human form and entered human affairs at times of special danger in order to preserve righteousness. In Hindu stories his two most famous visitations are in the form of Rama, the ideal king, and Krishna. Krishna is often pictured with cow girls, in particular one called Radha. Their relationship is seen as a supreme example of the love between Brahman and the human race.

Other popular gods are Kali, the mother goddess, Hanuman, the monkey god, and Ganesha the elephant god who removes obstacles.

The Sacred Books

Hinduism has many sacred scriptures which are classified under two heads: *sruti* — that is, scriptures directly inspired by God (the Vedas, the Brahmanas, Upanishads) or *dmriti* — books by holy men or prophets (Epics, Puranas, Bhagavad Gita).

The most popular of Hindu scriptures is the Bhagavad Gita —

usually known as the Gita. It means 'Song of the Beloved' and is a dialogue between Arjuna and Krishna. Arjuna, sitting in his chairot before doing battle with his enemies, who are also his cousins, is appalled by the prospect and argues with his chariot driver Krishna who later begins to teach him. Slowly the truth dawns that this is no chariot driver but the Lord Krishna. The message of the Gita is complex but much hinges on love — for fellows and for God.

Caste

A mark of the social organizations of Hinduism has been the caste system. In all there are thousands of sub-castes but the classical division is into four main castes:

Brahmins — the priests
Kshatriyas — the warriors and rulers
Vaishyas — the agricultural workers and merchants
Sudras — the servants

Traditionally the castes were very separate and people for example always married within them but this rigidity is now much less marked. In fact, since 1951 in India it has been illegal to discriminate on the grounds of caste.

Outside the formal caste system are the so-called 'outcasts' or 'untouchables' whose fate it was to do all the unpleasant jobs. They were not allowed to enter any temple and were supposed to live only within touching distance of other 'untouchables'. Gandhi called them the children of God and did much to raise their status in Indian society.

Worship

As with other religions, Hinduism believes that God cannot be contained in temples. However, temples are very prominent in Hinduism because like images they are helpful. In one sense the temple is seen as the house of the god and worshippers will call in to pay their respects. There will also be elaborate ceremonies in the morning and the evening to raise the god from sleep and to put him away for the night. In the morning the image will be washed, anointed and garlanded. Incense will be burned and food placed in the presence. This could all happen in a temple in a remote Indian village or in a British industrial city.

Temples vary much in size and splendour but normally they would have three essential things: an image of the god, a canopy (normally a roof) to cover the god and a priest to tend the temple and to make the people's offering. In Britain, a temple may be a former church or a converted hall or house so it may be quite cramped. Very often there will be the images of a number of gods spread around the temple. Over the day there is likely to be a constant stream of worshippers visiting the god.

In temples away from India congregational worship (puja) has become an important element in Hindu practice in addition to private devotion. In Britain, for example, Sunday, the day when most are free of work, has become the day when many Hindus gather at the temple to worship together. In the temple there are no chairs or benches so worshippers sit on the floor. Much worship consists of the singing of hymns and, of course, in the larger temples, dancing. The use of fire runs through many of the rituals. An important element is arti, a tray with five lights. This is moved slowly in front of the images of the gods. The arti tray is then brought around among the worshippers who pass their hands over the flame and then pass their hands over their own heads. This is symbolic of receiving God's blessing. With Indian worship we also associate the burning of incense, the offering of flowers and the giving of prasad, a mixture of dried fruit and sugar, which is the gift of God.

Devout Hindus will have a shrine within their homes, perhaps a corner of a room, which will have statues or pictures of gods. This will provide a focus for daily prayers. In India some families will have a priest to perform these ceremonies properly.

Festivals

There are many festivals in Hinduism; in fact there are so many gods (or manifestations of God) that at almost any given moment there would be a festival of some sort somewhere. Here there will be a focus on two of the best known festivals: Divali and Holi.

Divali often referred to as the 'Festival of Light', is perhaps the most popular Hindu festival. It lasts for five days and is marked by masses and masses of lights decorating temples, homes, buildings and so on. The festival is associated with the giving of presents and with parties. There are fireworks and much enjoyment. There are various stories which are attached to the festival: that Vishnu's consort, Lakshmi, brought gifts to homes for the coming year, Vishnu's defeat of the demon, Bali, and that it is the birthday of Kali. Whatever the connections it is a time of great exuberance, joy and *light*.

Holi is a spring festival celebrating the end of winter and the beginning of the season of growth. It is associated with bonfires and with coloured water and red powder. People spray each other with coloured water and throw red powder over each other. There is a story associated with it. King Hiranyakapishu, in his pride, ordered that all should worship him and him alone. His own son, Pralhad, defied this edict and continued to worship the Hindu gods. In anger his father tried to destroy him: to be trampled to death by an elephant, cast into a swollen river, thrown from a mountain and finally thrown into a great fire. None succeeded. Pralhad was unafraid because of his devotion to Vishnu. In his troubles he continued to chant the name of the god. Pralhad survived because he put his faith in God and chanted the divine names within the fire. This emphasizes the importance of simple trust in God. Many consider that the Holi bonfire commemorates that. Others say that it represents the death of the old year.

A Hindu's Life

The life of a Hindu is seen as a series of sixteen steps beginning before birth and ending after death. Each step is sanctified by an act of dedication to God. These sixteen steps divide into four stages. Each of the four stages is marked by suitable and appropriate activities.

The first stage is one of immaturity and the main task for the individual is to learn the traditions from one's elders.

The second stage is marked by marriage, by becoming a householder, by the parenting of children and the task of raising and supporting them and playing one's part in society.

The third quarter, with children grown up and independent, is marked by a great freedom from material cares and concerns. There is, therefore, more opportunity to spend time in thought, prayer and meditation. At one time it was not uncommon for people at this stage to leave to live in the peace of the forests.

The fourth quarter is the gradual edging out of life and a turning of heart and mind to meditation. This would be adopting the life of a monk, even perhaps a mendicant.

Many Hindus will, of course, not pass through all four stages.

Many will remain in stage two while others will move straight from stage one to stage four. In this latter group are the *guru* who teaches disciples the understanding and techniques to achieve liberation, the *sadhu* who practices the path of sainthood and the *swami*, the respected monk.

Initiation Ceremonies

After birth a baby is bathed, prayed over by the priest and placed on his father's knee. Then the sacred syllable AUM (the divine name) is traced on the baby's tongue with a pointed object dipped in honey and prayers are said over it concerning the future shape of life. For the first ten days of life the mother and child refrain from most human contact but on the twelfth day the child is named. Dressed in new clothes and placed in a swinging cot, twelve lamps are placed under the cot and the priest pronounces the name chosen by the family. Those present sing songs which incorporate the new name. The ceremony is followed by parties and gold and silver ornaments are often bought. Sometimes the child's ears are also pierced. Traditionally a boy's name should have an even number of syllables while a girl's should have an odd number.

During the third year (though some authorities say that it should happen just after the first birthday) the child's hair is cut. If this injunction is followed rigidly, the child's head is shaved. However, many parents are content with a short trim! The idea behind this is to make the sign that all bad karma from a previous existence is removed.

A very important step, the tenth, takes place normally between the ages of 8 and 12 years according to the caste of the child. It applies only to boys of the three highest castes: the priestly, warrior and merchant. The step is an initiation when the boy is deemed ready to begin a study of the Vedas, the sacred scriptures. This is also an important social event and there is usually a party to celebrate the occasion with the giving of presents. The one who is to be the boy's teacher or guru hangs a sacred thread over the boy's left shoulder and across his chest. The guru now takes responsibility for the boy's spiritual training. Not long after this the boy begins to study the Vedas. Very few boys now undertake the full traditional Vedic training which lasts twelve years. Most do a modified form of training.

Marriage

The second stage of life is that of the householder and involves the raising and supporting of a family. Marriages in India are usually arranged by the parents of the couple. They will seek to find a suitable match often in consultation with a priest. Thorough investigations are made. Brides should not be less than 16 years of age and bridegrooms are normally some years older.

The first step is betrothal. The bridegroom's family goes to visit the bride's family and exchanges coconuts as symbols of agreement. The date for the wedding is fixed at this meeting.

On the day of the wedding itself, the festivities begin with the formal giving of the bride by her father to the bridegroom by the bride's hand being placed in the bridegroom's. Presents are exchanged and the bridegroom gives the bride new clothes.

After this stage the guests begin to sing hymns which call down blessings upon the couple. While the singing is going on two wooden boards are placed near the centre of the hall and a curtain is held between. The couple are garlanded with flowers, brought to stand on the two boards facing each other but unable to see each other because of the curtain. At the end of each verse the congregation scatters rice over the couple. When the curtain is removed the couple exchange garlands and then sit side by side before the sacred fire.

Before the sacred fire the couple make offerings and walk around it. Prayers are made for their happiness and for their fruitfulness. The bride's sari is tied formally to the end of the husband's clothes in a knot and he takes seven steps which she follows one by one.

Wedding feasts are as splendid and elaborate as the bride's family can afford. They can also be the cause of debt in many Indian families. After the feasts the bride leaves her father's house and travels with her husband to his family home. In the doorway is placed a pot containing wheat. As he enters the bride kicks this over spilling the wheat over the floor. This is an expression of hope that the family will never lack an adequate supply of food.

Death

On death the body of a Hindu is washed, anointed and dressed in new clothes in preparation for cremation. Traditionally this was performed in a Kunda (a cremation spot) near a river and the body would be placed on a pyre. Nowadays many are cremated in modern crematoria.

Prayer is offered that the soul of the deceased person now released from the body may go to that stage which its karma merits. Often relatives will collect the ashes on the third day and either bury them or place them in a river. So the Hindu dies but unless his karma is such that he has achieved moksha (release) he is still on the wheel of existence and the round of birth and death will continue.

Islam

The religion known as Islam began about 1350 years ago in Arabia. The founder was Mohammed though he is seen only as a prophet, the one through whom God (Allah) spoke. Muslims (*never* to be called Mohammedads, as they follow God not Mohammed) see their religion stretching back long before then, from Abraham through the Old Testament prophets, through Jesus, to Mohammed, the final and greatest of the prophets.

What Do Muslims Believe and Do?

At the centre of Islam is submission to God. Islam means 'submission' and the true Muslim submits to the will of God. All Muslims accept five duties:

- (i) to believe solely in one God and that Mohammed is his prophet;
- (ii) to pray five times each day;
- (iii) to give alms;
- (iv) to fast during the month of Ramadan;
- (v) to go on a pilgrimage to Mecca at least once in one's life (if possible).

These are often called the *five pillars* of Islam.

There is No God but Allah and Mohammed is his Prophet

Muslims are strictly *monotheistic*. 'There is no God but Allah'. He is 'the One'. He has many other names given in the Koran; Muslims talk of the Ninety-nine Beautiful Names of God. He is known as the Lord, the High, the Great, the Creator, the Lifegiver, the Sustainer, the Compassionate, the Merciful. So great is He above all human understanding that all images or pictures of Him are forbidden as they would only diminish Him, hence the absence of human form in much Islamic art. He is seen as supreme over all, the loving provider and the just judge. Soon after birth any baby born into the Muslim community has the sacred text whispered into its ears 'God is most Great'.

Mohammed

Though in no way divine, Mohammed is regarded above any other human. As the greatest of the prophets and God's final mouthpiece, Mohammed is held in such respect that when Muslims speak his name they add 'May the peace and blessings of God be upon him'. It would be unthinkable that he would be depicted in art or in the cinema.

Mohammed was born in 570 AD in the city of Mecca (now in Saudi Arabia). An orphan from an early age, he was brought up by his uncle, and when the time came for him to find employment he became agent to a wealthy widow Khadijah, 15 years his senior, whom he later married. During his travels as agent for Khadijah, Mohammed came into contact with other religious groups, Christians and Jews, and was attracted by their religion. From the age of 40 onwards, Mohammed began to have visions of the Archangel Gabriel which he took, after some encouragement, to come from God. The main message of the visions was that he was the 'messenger of God' and that he was ordered to 'recite' the words of God which were coming to him. This recitation was the beginning of the Koran (which means recitation), the sacred book.

Mohammed's proclamation gained some converts but evoked considerable hostility from many fellow citizens so much so that Mohammed and his faithful band had to flee to Medina, a nearby city. However, Mohammed reentered Mecca in triumph in 630 AD, two years before his death in 632.

The Koran

The sacred book is treated with tremendous respect by Muslims because it is seen as being the *words of God*. It does not contain the words of Mohammed. He may have spoken them but only as a cypher. He recited God's words and they were heard by his disciples memorized and later written down. Since the Koran was spoken in Arabic, it has remained in that language since there is a deep fear that the translation of it might change its meaning.

The Koran is therefore perceived as the *final* revelation of God's will for the human race and it contains within it the *guidelines* for how life ought to be lived. This tends to be presented in general principles. More detailed instructions tend to be in the Traditions, the *Hadith*, which have grown up over a period of time and which therefore do not have the same status as the Koran.

Because of this significance attributed to the Koran, many Muslims learn the Koran by heart in Arabic, and learn Arabic too so as to understand it. Many mosques run schools to help children to learn the Koran. Many Muslim children in school in Britain will go to the mosque on several evenings each week to spend a couple of hours studying the Koran.

Prayer

It is laid down upon all Muslims to pray five times each day: just before sunrise, after midday, in the late afternoon, just after sunset and before midnight. Mosques have a chart of clock faces to indicate the exact times for prayer on a particular day. In a Muslim country a muezzin will mount the minaret of the mosque and call the faithful to prayer. Muslims are therefore reminded constantly of the greatness of God and the need to turn to him in prayer.

Preparation is needed for prayer. Muslims will wash thoroughly — hands, mouth, nose, face, arms, head, ears and feet, the outward washing being symbolic of inner cleansing. In prayer itself, there is a routine of both words and body movements. The set prayers can be said in any place provided it is clean; the worshipper merely unrolls his prayer mat, takes off the shoes and faces Mecca.

Although prayer can be said anywhere, most Muslims prefer to offer it at home or in the *mosque*.

Mosque means a place of *prostration*, for here Muslims bow their heads to the ground in acts of worship. As buildings mosques vary considerably. Some, in areas where Muslims are recent settlers, are converted houses or even factories, others are buildings of considerable splendour. Whatever they are they are basically places of shelter from the climate to enable Muslims to gather for worship, especially on Fridays and on festivals, and to be places of instruction in the Holy Koran for the young.

Mosques tend to be almost completely unfurnished. There are no chairs as this would inhibit the normal means of prayer — only a large floor space, usually carpeted. The only piece of furniture is likely to be a pulpit from which the Friday sermon is preached. Prayers in the mosque are often lead by an Imam, a minister employed to lead worship and to teach the faith. In one of the walls, there will be a small alcove (a mihrab) which indicates the direction of Mecca. The sexes are separated for prayer. Women are placed in balconies, or at the back of the mosque behind the men or sometimes in a separate room. The usual reason given is to reduce distractions! Because of the Prophet's strong objection to statues or pictures it is extremely rare to come across any in a mosque.

Almsgiving

An important teaching of Islam is that all humans are brothers and sisters and that one way in which this is recognized is through required almsgiving. All Muslims are required to give 2½ per cent of their earnings to charity, to the poor, needy, widows and so on. This is generally obeyed and in non-Muslim countries, Muslims may be giving their donations (zakat) over and above normal income tax.

Fasting

Fasting is a feature of most religions and is a way of asserting the control of the spiritual over the material in an individual. In Islam, the ninth month of the year, Ramadan, is dedicated to fasting. Muslims can fast at any time but all are *required* to do so in Ramadan. This means that for the twenty-nine or so days of the month, Muslims must not partake of food or drink between dawn and dusk. Ramadan comes at different times of the year and can be a real hardship during summer. Eating is allowed at night and in a Muslim community there is often a party atmosphere after dusk, with sweets and singing. All food and drink required must be consumed at night because at dawn — when it is possible to distinguish a dark thread from a light thread — the fast recommences. Children under 10, the old and sick, pregnant women, travellers and soldiers are exempted.

Pilgrimage to Mecca

All Muslims are urged to make once in their lives, the Major Pilgrimage, the Hajj, to Mecca. Because of the expense, many have to deny themselves this privilege. Mecca, because of its associations with the Prophet, is the holiest spot on earth for Muslims. The pilgrimage officially lasts for three days, during which the pilgrims visit the Kaaba, a hugh cube shaped building in the centre of the Great Mosque, Mount Safa and Mount Marwa, Mount Arafat and Mina. An interesting and essential feature of the Hajj is that all pilgrims must remove their normal clothing and don special clothing. In the case of a male pilgrim the special clothing consists of two pieces of white unsown cloth, one to go round the waist, down to the ankles, and the other to be placed over the shoulder. For women there is a single piece of cloth which covers the whole body. The only footwear permitted is a backless sandal. The purpose is to stress equality, and brotherhood and self sacrifice.

Festivals

The major festivals of Islam are the two Eids: the Eid ul Fitr and the Eid ul Adha.

The Eid ul Fitr, which means technically the lesser festival, is the more popular. It celebrates the end of the month long fast of Ramadan and is therefore a time of relaxation and rejoicing. It is a day of visiting, having parties, or wearing best clothes and of exchanging gifts and cards. Often a special sweet pudding made with milk and dates is served. If possible too the day includes visits to the graves of dead relatives.

The Eid ul Adha, the great festival, commemorates the ending of the Hajj, the pilgrimage to Mecca. It is kept not just by those in Mecca but by Muslims worldwide. It centres round a feast for which animals are sacrificed in the ritual way (halal). An individual family may present a lamb or goat, seven families may come together and provide a cow. Part of the meat is given away, mainly to the poor.

Birth, Marriage and Death

Birth

When a child is born, whether at home or in hospital, the sacred tenets of Islam are whispered into its ears. Although clearly there can be no understanding, it is felt important that the earliest words heard should concern God and his nature.

Marriage

In Islam marriage is often a simple and brief affair. Marriages are normally arranged, though consent from both parties is important. It may well be that the parties go to the mosque and in the presence of four witnesses recite passages from the Koran and repeat (three times) their consent to the marriage. In Britain it often happens that only the bridegroom will attend the service in the mosque. The bride would remain at home and be represented by an agent and probably two witnesses who could act on her behalf. They would hear her agreement (made three times) to the marriage and they would repeat this at the mosque when the Imam (minister) asked if she was willing. If both sides agree, then they are married. British law requires that there is also a civil ceremony.

Presents are exchanged but, more importantly, the dowry is negotiated and fixed. It is essential that a wife and children are maintained properly and this should be sorted out at the beginning. Divorce is possible but is disapproved of. There are several procedures laid down which are aimed at settling differences before a divorce is permitted.

Death

There is no one particular set way of burying the dead in Islam though there are common patterns. After death, the body is washed with sweet smelling soaps and spices before being wrapped in the shroud in which it will be buried. Bodies are buried ideally on the day following death in a grave slightly raised above the ground with the face turned to the right and facing Mecca. Relatives and friends meet together for the funeral either at the house or at the mosque. The funeral is generally an ordinary salat but includes prayers for the dead one. Inevitably funeral customs will vary where Muslims are minority groups. It is often not possible in Britain to arrange for the funeral to be on the day after death and most cemeteries insist that bodies are placed in coffins.

Judaism

The Jewish faith is of ancient origin claiming such early leaders as Abraham and Moses. It also gave birth, in a sense, to both Christianity and Islam. It is small in numbers of adherents as it is made up largely of Jews born into it through the female line. It does have converts from outside Jewry but while it accepts them it does not especially seek them. By no means all people who are Jewish by birth accept the practice of Judaism and within those who do there are various degrees of practice.

Shema

Judaism is based upon belief in the unity of God. This is summed up in The Shema (Deuteronomy, chapter 6, verse 4) 'Hear, O Israel, the Lord our God is *one* Lord'.

This Lord who is one is also creator and sustainer of the universe, continually active within it. Yet this same Lord is in relationship with mankind: the Shema continues 'and thou shalt love the Lord your God with all your heart and with all your soul and with all your might'. There is intimacy in the relationship: many Jewish prayers talk to God as *Father*.

Judaism places great emphasis upon faith and trust in the loving purposes of God. More than any other religious group, Jews have suffered over the centuries, especially under the Nazis. Yet many have kept their faith in God's good purposes and lived without bitterness. *The Diary of Anne Frank* written while she, a teenage girl, was in hiding from the Nazis in occupied Holland, is a very powerful example of this.

The Ten Commandments

Judaism believes that its relationship with God is based upon a Covenant. 'I will be your God and you will be my people'. The human side of the relationship is to keep God's law, which finds its central expression in the Ten Commandments:

1. I am the Lord thy God.
2. Thou shalt have no other gods before me.
3. Thou shalt not take the Lord's name in vain.
4. Remember the Sabbath Day to keep it holy.
5. Honour thy father and mother.
6. Thou shalt not murder.
7. Thou shalt not commit adultery.
8. Thou shalt not steal.
9. Thou shalt not bear false witness against thy neighbour.
10. Thou shalt not covet.

By living in this way, Judaism is a vehicle for demonstrating God's righteousness and his justice to the world. The Commandments also show very clearly Judaism's commitment both to loving and serving God and also its commitment to one's neighbours.

The Synagogue and the Home

The synagogue (literally, place of meeting or gathering) and the home work together in teaching the law, and consequently the way of holiness.

The synagogue is the focal point of religious training and worship for the Jewish community. The focal point of the synagogue is the Ark; this is the receptacle which holds scrolls of the five books of Moses. The Ark is placed on the east wall of the synagogue facing towards Jerusalem. In the centre of the synagogue or near to the Ark is a raised platform, the bimah, to which the scrolls are brought for public reading. A light burns perpetually before the Ark. The reading from the Scrolls of the Law form the centre of Sabbath worship and members of the congregation are called up for the honour of reading. This all emphasizes the centrality of the law in Judaism. Male worshippers usually wear a small skull cap, the yarmulka, and a prayer shawl called a tallith. In Orthodox synagogues, women play little part in the service and often sit in a balcony.

In the home too there is strong emphasis upon bringing the children up well and Jewish families are traditionally close and warm. The fifth commandment requires children to honour their parents. Parents are expected in return to give their children a good example. Again the emphasis is upon the Law. Many Jewish homes have a *Mezuzah* attached to the right hand doorpost of the house and on those of the living room. The *Mezuzah* is a small case containing a tiny parchment scroll on which the first two paragraphs of the Shema are inscribed. It obeys the command of Deuteronomy, chapter 11, verse 20, 'And thou shalt write them upon the door posts of thine house and upon thy gates'. The *Mezuzah* is there as a permanent sign that the law should be observed in the whole of life. Women occupy a key position in the home and it is there that their powerful influence is felt most. The home too is the place where much of the religion is practised. Festivals like the Passover are celebrated mainly in the home. The day is (ideally) punctuated three times by prayer in the home. In the morning, at noon and in the evening. As he rises each morning a devout Orthodox Jew will put on his yarmulka, the tallith and strap on

An Introduction to Five Religions

the phylacteries or tefillin. These are a pair of black leather boxes, one of which is placed on the forehead and the other on the left forearm. They contain the words of the Shema. The practice arises out of the instruction in the book of Deuteronomy chapter 6, verse 8, 'And thou shalt bind them for a sign upon thine head, and they shall be as frontlets between thine eyes'. This literal interpretation emphasizes the importance attached in Judaism to the subjugation of the mind, the heart and the strength to God.

The Festivals and Holy Days

Judaism has a number of festivals and Holy Days. Those which are most likely to be discussed in school are probably:

The Sabbath

The fourth commandment orders Jews to keep holy the Sabbath Day — the seventh day of the week (Saturday). There should be a cessation of labour, a change from the other six days. This is often seen as a negative thing (not switching on electric lights and so on) as a day of restrictions but this misses the heart of the commandment. The Sabbath is intended to be a joy, a delight, a time of moving nearer to God and a respite from worry and concern.

The Passover

The first of the three pilgrim festivals (the others being Weeks and Tabernacles) is the spring festival which celebrates the freeing of the children of Israel from Egypt. The family and guests gather round for the Passover meal. The youngest person asks the ancient question, 'Why is this night different from all other nights?' and then the president of the meal replies 'We were slaves under Pharaoh in the land of Egypt and God brought us forth out of Egypt'. During the meal there are the symbols of the Exodus: the bitter herbs symbolizing the anguish of slavery and the unleavened bread (*matzoh*) which the Israelites had to make quickly and called the bread of affliction.

The New Year and Day of Atonement

The Jewish New Year inaugurates ten days of penitence: they are described in Hebrew as the 'Ten days of return'. They should be used for the examination of behaviour and life over the past year, for prayers for forgiveness and for a working at restoring harmony in our dealings with God and with our fellows. The New Year begins with an assertion of the Kingship of God and the *shofar* or ram's horn is blown in the synagogue as a call to return to God.

The Day of Atonement, the tenth day, is considered the holiest day of the Jewish Year. No food or drink is taken. The key notes of the day are true penitence, confession and real reconciliation. Despite this it is not a day of gloom, as symbolized by the white robes of the rabbi. The day ends with the congregation repeating after the rabbi the ancient prayer: 'Hear O Israel the Lord our God, the Lord is One; Blessed be his name whose glorious kingdom is forever and ever'. Then the congregation repeats seven times 'The Lord, he is God'.

The *shofar* is again blown as a reminder that the spirit of the Day of Atonement should continue throughout the year.

Chanukkah

This is a winter festival and falls close to Christmas. It celebrates the victory of Judas Maccabeus in the second century BC. Emperor Antiochus Epiphanes of Syria, whose empire included Palestine, ordered that all his terrritories should adopt the gods of Greece. To devout Jews this was an impossible demand and they resisted. Antiochus Epiphanes strengthened his resolve and forbade the practice of Judaism. The temple itself was desecrated and in its holiest place was erected a statue of Zeus. Despite the persecutions (described in the Book of the Macabees in the Apocrypha), many faithful Jews stood firm. Although their numbers were very small over against the might of Antiochus, they won through. It is this courageous group who through their faith in God preserved the Faith.

It is said that when Judas Maccabeus and his people repossessed the temple and cleansed it there was only one jar of pure oil remaining, enough to keep the temple candelabrum alight for one night. By a miracle the oil lasted for eight days.

Chanukkah was established to celebrate the cleansing and rededication of the temple. Each year in home and synagogue a light is lit on the first night of the festival and another on each evening until eight are lit.

An Introduction to Five Religions

Celebrations

Barmitzvah

Jewish children are normally taught about their religion from an early age and many learn Hebrew because it is the language of the Bible and the prayer books. At the age of 13 a Jewish boy attains religious maturity and is known as Barmitzvah (literally, 'son of the law'). On the Sabbath nearest to his thirteenth birthday he will be called up in the synagogue to recite from the scrolls. In the sermon the rabbi will address him and pronounce on him the Lord's blessing. There is, of course, much social celebrating too at such an event. The boy has become an adult member of the Jewish community. In many places now there is a similar event for girls, the bathmitzvah (literally, 'daughter of the law').

Marriage

Family life in Judaism is strongly cherished and marriage is seen as a solemn covenant. Before the ceremony, the bridegroom signs the marriage document in which he promises to be a loving and caring husband. He then stands with his father under the canopy, a large square of embroidered material supported by four poles. Then the bride with her family and attendants enters and joins the bridegroom under the canopy, which represents their future home. The bride and groom drink from a goblet and the bridegroom places a ring on the bride's forefinger. The final act of the marriage is for the bridegroom to break a glass under his foot. This custom is intended to represent that even in the pleasure and joy of life there is pain.

Death

Although it is a religious duty to preserve life, when death comes it is accepted and the ceremonies which are performed are designed (as in most faiths) to comfort and strengthen the bereaved and to treat the dead with as much dignity as possible.

The body is washed and prepared for burial in a simple coffin. In the case of a Jewish male, the body is wrapped in a simple white shroud and the tallith. Burial is usually on the day following death or as soon as possible after that. Cremation is permitted by some Jewish congregations. The prayers used are full of praise for God.

Because burial is so soon after death, mourning comes after the funeral. The first week is a time of intense mourning (called shivah) — the family basically remains at home and is visited by friends who come to commiserate and console. For the first year after death, the family will make a point of being present to join in Kaddish at the synagogue. Kaddish is the act of sanctification made near to the end of the service. It is traditional to observe the anniversary of a death by the lighting of candles in the home and of saying Kaddish in the synagogue.

Sikhism

Sikhism points to *Guru Nanak* (1469–1539 AD) as its founder. Guru Nanak lived in India and was concerned about the rivalry between Hindus and Muslims. His great concern was to enable people to see the truth about God which was to be found in *both* Islam and Hinduism. Tradition has it that when Nanak was on his death bed, both Hindus and Muslims came to claim his body. Nanak instructed them to place fresh cut flowers by him, the Hindus on his right and the Muslims on his left. Whichever flowers remained fresh on the following morning would signify to whom his body belonged. Then, Nanak covered himself with a sheet. Next morning, his body was gone but both lots of flowers were fresh!

Nanak intended to found no new religion but inevitably his followers formed a new group and he had to appoint a new guru to succeed him.

A Sikh means 'one who learns', that is one who learns to know God through the gurus. A guru is a religious teacher.

The Guru Granth Sahib

Nanak was the first of the ten gurus of Sikhism. God is the true guru; Nanak and his successors are the human instruments through whom he speaks. The tenth guru, Gobind Singh, indicated that after his death there would be no further human guru. Instead there would be a collection of scriptures, consisting of the teaching of the gurus, the Guru Granth Sahib.

Tremendous respect is accorded the Guru Granth Sahib. It is the central focus of the Gurdwara (temple) (literally 'the door of the guru'). It is placed there on a raised platform on cushions and covered by a canopy. When people enter the Gurdwara, they remove their shoes, cover their head and go straight to the Guru Granth Sahib. There they bow down right to a kneeling position, the head touching the ground. Offerings of money or of food are usually made: it is very common to see a bag of apples or a bottle of milk before the platform!

Most Sikh worship consists of the reading of the Granth and the singing of hymns. The reader sits cross-legged behind the Granth, in his hand a chavri, made from animal hairs, which he waves over the sacred book. In every way, the Granth is treated like a living guru. All the important events of life occur before the Granth: the naming of a child, marriage, initiation as an adult.

Some Sikh families have a copy of the Granth at home though it would not be kept on a bookshelf like a Bible might. It would normally be kept in a room set aside for the purpose. Sikhs would normally bathe before entering the room and would enter in reverence, shoeless and with heads covered. Many Sikh families do not have their own copy because they are not able to give it the proper treatment it should have.

This provides a caution for teachers who might ask Sikh pupils to bring a copy of the Granth to school. This involves making the classroom into a Gurdwara for the time that it is on the premises: it is much easier to take the children out to the proper Gurdwara!

The Khalsa (The Brotherhood)

It was the tenth guru, Gobind Singh, who formed the Sikhs into a soldier brotherhood. This is known as the Khalsa. As a sign of equal brotherhood within it all males are given the surname Singh (Lion) and all females kaur (Princess). A military discipline was imposed upon them: all Sikhs are expected to rise, bathe (normally in cold water) and pray before dawn.

The Brotherhood is to be distinguished by five features of dress. Because all five begin with the letter K they are called the 5 Ks.

  (i)   The *Kesh* (long uncut hair): all Sikhs were ordered not to cut their hair. This symbolizes spirituality.
  (ii) The *Kangha* (comb): the long hair was not to be unruly but kept clean and in order, symbolize by the comb.
  (iii) The *Kirpan* (sword): all Sikhs were to carry a sword, to fight for truth and righteousness. This among Sikhs in the United Kingdom is almost always now a symbolic sword and may even be a sword brooch.

(iv) The *Kachs* (shorts): these are short trousers worn by men and women and which were much more suited to battle than the long trousers often worn.
(v) The *Kara* (the bracelet): all Sikhs are supposed to wear a steel bracelet on their right wrist. Practically it may have at one time served as a protection against bow strings. It also has the great symbolism of eternity and unity. It symbolizes the eternity and unity of God and also the unity between Sikh and Sikh and Sikh and God.

It may seen odd that what is perhaps the most visible mark of a Sikh male, the turban, does not appear on this list. Nevertheless it is greatly cherished by Sikhs.

Amrit (Initiation)

All those who wish to be initiated into the Sikh religion and to become members of the Khalsa do so in the Amrit ceremony. This takes place in front of the Guru Granth Sahib. Five members of the Khalsa dressed in yellow tunics with a red or yellow sash over the right shoulder stand with them. These five mix water and sugar in a steel bowl, stirring it with a sword, reciting hymns as they do it. This is the *Amrit*. Then one by one those wishing to be initiated come forward and kneel. Each one in turn is given the mixture five times to drink, five times it is splashed in the eyes and five times sprinkled upon the head. Then the initiate makes certain vows, for example, not to smoke tobacco or to take harmful drugs and always to display the five Ks. By no means all Sikhs undergo initiation.

Hospitality

The brotherhood of Sikhs is expressed very profoundly by the Gurdwara. Not only are all Sikhs equal before God in the Gurdwara but this is emphasized by the sharing of the *karah parshad* at every service. This is a mixture of flour (or sometimes, semolina) sugar, butter and water which forms a sweet pudding. Each worshipper takes a little in his or her hands and eats it. Attached to each Gurdwara are also kitchens and places to eat. To be hospitable to fellow Sikhs and indeed to all people is very important in Sikhism and many English visitors to a Gurdwara will find that they will be offered tea and biscuits as a minimum, and, if they arrive at the right time, curry and chapattis! On a festival, a Gurdwara may feed many thousands of worshippers.

Festivals

Anniversaries of the gurus are called *Gurpurbs*. The principal ones commemorate the birthdays of Guru Nanak and Guru Gobind Singh and the martyrdoms of Guru Arjan and Guru Tegh Bahadur. Normally before each Gurpurb there is a continuous reading of the Guru Granth (this takes about forty-eight hours) followed on the morning of the Gurpurb by services in the Gurdwara. In India there would normally be a procession of the Guru Granth through the town drawn on a vehicle decorated with flowers and bunting. This procession does not happen in Britain.

Sikhs keep other festivals drawn from Hinduism but often with a different significance, especially Divali and Baisakhi.

Birth, Marriage and Death

Birth

There are no specific ceremonies associated with birth, but as soon as the mother is well enough she brings her baby to the Gurdwara. There, before the Guru Granth Sahib, the parents make gifts and prayers are said for long life for the child. The concluding prayer contains the following lines:

> I present this child and with Thy Grace
> I administer to him the Amrit
> May he be a true Sikh
> May he devote himself to the service of his
> Fellow men and his motherland
> May he be inspired with devotion.

Then Amrit (sugar and water) which has been prepared is offered, a drop is placed on the baby's lips and the remainder is drunk by the mother. Then the Granth is opened at random and the first hymn on the left hand page read out. Whatever is the first letter of the first word of the hymn should be the initial letter of the baby's name. If it is 'g' the baby may be called Gurdeep, if it is 'm' the baby may be called

Malkit. At the end of the service, the *karah parshad* is shared around again as a sign of brotherhood.

Marriage

Normally a Sikh marriage is an arranged match. The only essential witness is the Guru Granth Sahib and it is before it that the marriage takes place. It may be in the Gurdwara or in the bride's home. In the Gurdwara, the couple would sit in front of the Guru Granth Sahib, the bride usually dressed in red. The couple and their fathers stand while the Granthi, the leader of the worship, asks for their consent and for the agreement of the gathered congregation. There is a symbolic touch whereby the edge of the bride's sari or her headdress is tied to the bridegroom's sash. The wedding hymn is chanted from the Guru Granth Sahib a verse at a time and then sung. During the chanting of a verse the couple stand before the Granthi and then while it is being sung they walk around the Guru Granth Sahib slowly in a clockwise direction. This takes place four times, once for each verse. The service concludes, as do all services, with the sharing of the *karah parshad*.

Death

Death is seen by Sikhs as the means whereby the faithful pass into the presence of God. Extravagant mourning or wailing is not encouraged, though for ten days after a funeral the family will read through the Guru Granth Sahib, alone and when friends visit them. The normal pattern is for a body to be washed and dressed and then placed in a shroud in preparation for cremation on the same day as death or the next day. If cremation is not possible then the body is buried.

7 Teaching World Religions

Attitudes to the teaching of world religions, other than Christianity, vary considerably. Here are a few representative ones:

> They (i.e. the children) have enough difficulty understanding their own so I don't see how they are going to understand very different ones.

> I think that as they live in a multi-cultural society the sooner they begin to understand that people have different beliefs the better.

> I'm not happy about it. There is so little time, not enough to get into Christianity.

> I think religious education is about religion and religion is broader than Christianity.

> I think that it's good for children to see that people all over the world are committed to religion — and not just that funny lot at the church down the road.

Within these views it is easy to detect a number of underlying attitudes. There is the lingering notion that the real aim of religious education is still confessional and that we should, therefore, be using all our energy in commending Christianity. In such a view, a study of other religions is something of a distraction and wasting of time. There is also the fear of confusing children — religious ideas from others are too difficult for young children! Much depends here upon which dimensions one chooses to present. Clearly the doctrinal dimensions of religions would be inappropriate but not those which deal with the more concrete aspects, the social and ritual dimensions nor the mythological dimension which deals with the stories.

Children through books, magazines, newspapers and television are aware from quite a young age of the existence of different religions in the world, even if they do not have first-hand experience of them. They are certainly starting to ask questions about them by the age of 8. If they live in a multi-religious area and rub shoulders in school with children from different religious traditions then the questions come even earlier.

Given the approach to religious education outlined in chapter 2 it follows that religious education should be concerned with a variety of religions. The only reservation would be its suitability conceptually for the child. If material was being presented to children which they were not able to understand, then however desirable it was, it would be a pointless activity. However, enough teaching of world religions has taken place with younger children for us to know that it can be used valuably and purposefully. The crucial question, as it is in the teaching of Christianity, is the *selection* of appropriate material.

At what age then should work on world religions be introduced? Here much depends on the first-hand experiences of the child. If young children come into contact with the externals of other religions, if they are in class with Sikh boys with plaited hair or with children whose mothers wear shalwars, then questions will come early and the teacher can begin the task of explaining. If the child has no first-hand contact in this way then most schools would normally not introduce such material until the age of eight or so.

One teacher, now very enthusiastic but originally suspicious of the introduction of other religions into the education of young children, records his conversion:

> It was on a cold Monday morning, when I was collecting money from my 8 and 9-year-olds for school lunches for the week, that our one and only Muslim pronounced that she hadn't brought any dinner money that week because she wasn't going to have any school lunches for a month. This information was greeted with cries of horror and disbelief from those gathered around my desk. 'What not for a whole month. You'll die of starvation' and so on. Fortunately it occurred to me that Ramadan was due to start about that time so I got Karim to explain. Very quietly she told what was now the whole class listening that for one month in the year, Muslims were supposed not to eat or drink anything in the hours of daylight and that the month had begun the day before. Although, because it was cold and she was quite young she could have

been exempted from the fast, she had wanted to join in and her father had agreed.

This revelation proved the day's topic of absorbing interest. It kept bubbling up at what seemed every other minute with questions addressed to me like 'We don't do things like that, do we?' and various comments made sotto voce 'It's mad'.

It was the combination of these two comments that made me feel that the class ought to be doing some work on other religions. And so we began — on a topic on 'How people worship'. What amazed me was how well it went. There was none of the boredom that some colleagues predicted. Rather the interest in and the quality of the work — research in the library, written work, art work — was exceptionally high — much higher for this work than for any other unit of work done over the year. The school was situated in what is often called a 'deprived' area.

Possible Approaches

5–9 Years

Multiracial schools

If the school serves a religiously-mixed neighbourhood there will be much religious education going on incidentally. Children will absorb some of the things which children from other religions do and will ask questions: 'Why doesn't Manjit have his hair cut?', 'Why does Kamaljit's mother have a red spot on her forehead?'. The teacher will want to deal with these questions as they arise and will often want to involve not just the questioner but a group of children, perhaps the whole class, including the child about whom the question is asked. Very much of the work done on world religions with young children in such schools will take this form. This underlines two important matters.

Firstly, class teachers in multiracial schools need to be knowledgeable about the religious and cultural background of the children they teach. This is a professional matter and such understanding might well affect the way a teacher deals with a pupil in certain situations. In addition to this it is immensely cheering and encouraging to both parents and children from ethnic minorities to know that schools will make this effort. Sometimes a teacher is heard to say, 'I'm not interested in all that. As far as I'm concerned they're all children and all children are the same'. While it is possible to recognize an important insight in this remark it is ultimately a very inadequate attitude because it ignores much of what is significant to the children and their learning.

Secondly, teachers need to be sensitive to the attitudes which they are conveying to the children in their care, both from the host and from the minority communities. The teacher who explained to her class that there was a religious rule which required Sikh boys to 'let their hair grow long like girls not like our boys who have it cut' was in a small way helping to foster unhelpful attitudes. Firstly she was helping to create a mocking attitude towards Sikhs and Sikh customs among white children in the class and secondly she was causing acute embarrassment among the Sikh boys over one of their distinctive marks. Part of the work of religious education is to foster attitudes of interest, tolerance and respect which are all essential to the growth of sympathetic understanding of religions and their adherents. And these attitudes begin to form very early in life.

A fruitful approach of a planned kind which has been used successfully with young children is through festivals. It is not a cognitive approach to festivals, in which they are studied and discussed but rather through an enactment of them. If they are celebrated in the school and if the talents of pupils from minority groups can be harnessed to share their songs, dances, mimes, stories and music, then it is possible for young children to enter into them at the level of *feeling*. The children may not know very much about the festival but they can still feel what is being conveyed through ritual and symbol.

Here is an example of this:

> Last year at Divali we put a number of small lamps — some were night lights which we stood in jam jars surrounded by coloured tissue paper — on the tables in the school hall. The children came quietly and wide eyed into the hall for assembly while Indian classical music was being played ... We talked about fear of the dark how glad we are to have lights and how we burn candles at Christmas and at birthday parties when we are happy. In India, in October, the summer rains are over and people are happy because the skies are clear and they can see the stars at night. The festival of lights, called Divali, is held then and the story of Prince Rama is remembered. I told the story at assembly ... At the end of the story I said the following prayer: 'Dear God, thank you for the joy of light and

Teaching World Religions

candles and twinkling stars. Help us not to be afraid when it is dark, but to be brave and helpful to all your creatures as Prince Rama was'. We than sang the hymn 'All Things Bright and Beautiful' and afterwards the Asian children, each holding a candle, stood in the middle of the hall while we wished them 'A Happy Divali'. In this assembly, which lasted about a quarter of an hour, we recognized that joy, light and homecomings are experiences enjoyed by children of all faiths.[1]

This is no sense a full or clear understanding of Divali but it is a feeling towards it, and as such is a firm foundation upon which to build developing understanding.

With this age group there is probably little else that needs to be provided in the area of world religions. What happens will provide a useful basis for much more work at a later age.

Non-multiracial schools

The situation is quite different in schools where the children all have backgrounds in Christian culture. Children at this stage are much more interested in the here and now and much of their learning is related to, and stimulated by, their environment. Within that environment there are no adherents of other religions who will stimulate questions.

Most teachers do not feel it appropriate to raise the question of other religions at this age though some do include within the stories they tell examples from other cultures and religions. Perhaps the most popular topic which touches a little on material drawn from world religions is 'Children around the world'. Here small pieces of information may be included, for example, 'Abdul does not pray to God in a church but in a mosque', 'Malhit takes his shoes off when he goes into the temple'. Objections are often raised to topics like this because it is claimed that they present stereotyped images to children. This is probably true though it is often difficult to see how the problem can be avoided with this age group.

Normally, it would be unusual to see much work going on in world religions with younger children in this type of school though as children's understanding develops there will be more opportunities.

World Religions with Children Aged 9–12 Years

As children develop and their understanding is less tied to objects in their immediate experience, it becomes possible to introduce more material drawn from a variety of religious traditions. The growth of interest in this work both among those concerned about religious education and those concerned with multicultural education is evidenced by the greatly increased number of books available which are suited to children aged 8 years and older (see 'Resources').

Teachers can approach this work with children in a number of ways but three seem particularly fruitful.

One approach is to take one religion and to look at it either as a whole or at different aspects of it. A starting point might be 'What does it mean to be a Muslim'. This would involve looking at the different dimensions of Islam, the Koran, the festivals and so on. This might be done, if desired, by looking at Islam through the eyes of a Muslim boy or girl. Another starting point might be the study of Ramadan, probably at the time when it falls in the year, or one of the festivals. The teacher might also want to spend some sessions on studying the life of Mohammed himself.

A second approach is to take a theme which draws on material from a number of religious traditions. Here the teacher would be looking at similar aspects in different religions. Examples of themes are: Founders; How people worship; Temples, mosques and churches; festivals of Light (Divali, Christmas, Hannukah); Weddings; Initiation rites; Sacred books.

A third approach would be to encourage religious understanding from a theme which is not itself directly religious. Examples of this could be Bread, Light and Food.

Example 1 — A focus upon one religion
JUDAISM (for children aged nine years or older)
Aims

    (i) to approach Judaism with openness and respect;
    (ii) to give some knowledge of Judaism focussing in particular upon the ritual and social dimensions;
    (iii) to encourage the beginnings of an understanding of and empathy with Judaism;
    (iv) to begin to see Judaism as a way of life.

The following areas could be investigated:

The Jewish home and its importance in the practice of Judaism
The place of religion in the home
Lighting the Sabbath candles
The Passover meal

Mezuzah — the centrality of the Law in the home
Weddings — marriage as the basis of family life

The Sabbath
The special nature of the Sabbath
Origin in the Ten Commandments
Different ways of keeping the Sabbath
Sabbath worship in the synagogue

The synagogue
Preferably arrange a visit
Features of the synagogue — the Ark containing the scrolls of the Law, the bimah, the centrality of the Law
Customs in worship — the yamulkah, the tallith, phylacteries

Barmitzvah/Bathmitzvah (the coming of age of the boy/girl)
Coming of age at 13
The training of children in the knowledge of the Law and in the rudiments of the Hebrew language
Ceremonies in the synagogue, especially the child reading from the Law
Social and community celebrations
Responsibilities of adulthood

Festivals
Perhaps the most suitable one to concentrate upon would be Passover
Passover meal — what is said, what is eaten (a little historical explanation can be helpful)
Significance of the Passover for Jews

Judaism's stability (at the discretion of the teacher)
Judaism's continued existence after periods of intense persecution culminating in the Nazi attempt at genocide. It may be useful to talk about the life of Anne Frank and to read some extracts from her diary

Example 2 — A theme drawn from more than one religion
SACRED BOOKS (for children aged ten and upward)
Aims

    (i) to introduce children to the sacred written documents of several religions;
    (ii) to explore ways in which believers show respect and reverence for sacred books;

Religious Education 5-12

(iii) to help children to see the ways in which holy books are used in the context of religious worship;
(iv) to consider the influence of sacred books in the lives of believers;
(v) to consider some of the ways in which sacred books are compiled.

Possible approaches:

1. The identification and handling of a number of sacred books: the Koran (Islam), the Granth (Sikhism), the Torah (Judaism), the Bible (Christianity), the Bhavagad Gita (Hinduism). Familiarity with the names.
2. The association of sacred books with particular leaders: the Koran with the Prophet Mohammed, the Granth with Guru Nanak and the other nine gurus; the Bible with its many authors.
3. The idea of revelation — that these books are special because they reveal something of the divine in a special way, for example the visions of Mohammed and the experience of the Hebrew prophets.
4. Transmission of the scriptures
   Papyrus, vellum, manuscripts, scribes.
   The Dead Sea Scrolls
   The Scriptorum at Qumran
   Monastic copying, illuminated manuscripts, the Book of Kells
5. The notion of reverence — what does it mean?
   Treatment of sacred books
   the Granth in Sikhism — special room in the house
                         — special room in the gurdwara
                         — focus of worship
   the place of the Scrolls of the Law both in the synagogue and its worship
   the gospel procession in Christian worship and the special place given to reading from the Bible
6. The use of sacred books for understanding the divine
   Teaching about God
   Sacred stories
7. Sacred books as guides for living
   The ethical teaching of the various religions. For example: The Sermon on the Mount
   The centrality of the Law in Judaism — the 'mezuzah' and barmitzvah

Example 3 — An aspect of a theme which is not itself directly religious
FOOD
During a topic on 'food' which focussed mainly upon the different foods around the world, the different constituents of food and the food required for building healthy bodies, the teacher explored the importance of food in sharing and in binding people together.

Food is a very important element in religions. In Sikhism, for example, *karah parshad*, is shared among all the worshippers to show that they all belong together as one family. After the service, the worshippers gather together to share a full meal because they belong to the same family. In the Hindu Temple, worshippers bring gifts with them and rarely leave without a piece of fruit or some nuts. In Christianity, worship centres around the Holy Communion where worshippers gather round the altar to receive bread and wine.

The teacher took up these neglected social/religious aspects of food and incorporated them into the more normal topic.

Note

1   Wilson, E. (1970) 'World religions in the infants school', *Child Education*, Autumn.

8 An Extended Topic: Pilgrimage

Teacher's Material

Underlying most religions is the notion that life is a pilgrimage, an interior moving from what one is to what one ought to be and can become. John Bunyan in his *Pilgrim's Progress* tells the allegory of Christian's journey from his home in the City of Destruction to the Celestial City and relates what he encountered on the way. Beyond this in most religions, too, pilgrimage as a physical journey is a widespread phenomenon. Islam has the Hajj, the pilgrimage to Mecca which is one of its five pillars. Each year at Passover, Jews use the phrase 'next year in Jerusalem'. Hindus travel great distances to Benares to bathe in the Ganges. Christians make pilgrimage to Jerusalem to retrace the steps of Christ. Sikhism has a strong tradition which is against pilgrimages, though this does not prevent many Sikhs making pilgrimage.

Behind the notion of pilgrimage is the idea that certain places are special or, to use a religious term, holy (literally: set apart). That certain places have special significance is part of everyday experience. The couple who return each year on their wedding anniversary to a forest to locate a particular tree under which they agreed to marry are making a sort of pilgrimage. Devotees of Shakespeare who visit the sites associated with him in and around Stratford-upon-Avon are witnesses to the same phenomenon. So too are the Russians who queue all day in order to file silently past the embalmed body of Lenin in his mausoleum by the Kremlin walls.

In religious practice certain places are made sacred by history and by prayer and so they are marked off from the territory round about. In Judaism, for example, the land of Israel is sacred. In Jewish theology it is the promised land, given by God. In that sense it is marked off from every other piece of land. Within the promised land there are also

An Extended Topic: Pilgrimage

different degrees of specialness. Jerusalem occupies a special place in loyalty and affection. It housed the Temple and the Ark of the Covenant. In particular, now, of special significance is the Western Wall (usually known as the Wailing Wall), all that remains of Herod's great temple. This is special and sacred.

Sacred places are often associated with the 'founders' of religions. For Christians, for example, Jerusalem is pre-eminent because it was the scene of the most significant events in the life of Jesus. Here God walked! In Islam Mecca is intimately associated with Mohammed. In Hinduism Benares is associated with both the god, Shiva and the god, Rama. In Sikhism, the Golden Temple at Amritsar, built by the fifth guru, Arjan, is a place of special pilgrimage to many.

Many holy places are associated with special holy people or saints. In the Christian religion, for example, places associated with appearances of Mary, mother of Jesus, are very popular. Specially well known are the shrines at Fatima in Portugal, Guadalupe in Mexico, Knock in Ireland, Walsingham in England and, of course, most famous of all, Lourdes, in south-west France. A brief look at Lourdes will indicate another aspect of pilgrimage — the notion of being made whole.

Lourdes is a small town in the foothills of the Pyranees. In 1858 a 14-year old girl, Bernadette Soubirous, witnessed eighteen appearances of Mary at the Grotto of Massabiele. At first she was teased by her friends and her mother forbade her to go again to the Grotto for no-one else saw the 'lady, young and beautiful, exceedingly beautiful, the like of whom I have not seen before'. However, her simplicity and quiet persistence led them all to change their minds and after the visions ceased, she was able to convince the suspicious church authorities that she had indeed seen the Virgin. Mary did not appear again at Lourdes, nor indeed again to Bernadette but she left a spring of water which continues to flow. Bernadette herself became a nun, died in 1879 and was canonized in 1933. Long before Bernadette was canonized, Lourdes had become a great centre of pilgrimage. Many sick people came to bathe in the waters of the spring and there were many reported cures. The sick come in their hundreds of thousands each year to Lourdes and one of the most impressive sights for the visitor to Lourdes, whether as tourist or pilgrim, is to see the sick in their hundreds wheeled out on beds or in chairs to attend either a mass at the grotto or the Blessed Sacrament Procession. Naturally most of the sick hope deep down for a cure from their disease but the official view is that healing may take other forms and is, at root, about reconciliation with God. Lourdes is now the largest centre of Christian pilgrimage.

It is clear that pilgrimage is therefore a large scale activity within a number of religions and that many believers will put themselves to considerable expense, trouble and inconvenience to make them. In Chaucer's *Canterbury Tales*, which is itself set within the context of a pilgrimage from London to the shrine of the martyred archbishop, Thomas Becket, at Canterbury, it is revealed that one of the pilgrims, the wife of Bath, has also been on pilgrimage to the shrine of St. James at Compostello in Northern Spain and also to the Holy Land itself!

What makes a pilgrimage that rather than a sightseeing holiday? The answer seems to be in the attitude of the individual. Those who go to the holy place to stare are the tourists, those who go to worship are the pilgrims. The pilgrim's motive may be an expression of devotion, it may be an offering of thanks, it may be to seek the healing of body, mind and spirit. It may be to seek a bridge between the present and the past. Above all, though, it will be a desire to draw nearer to God, if only for a short time. That is the central motive of the pilgrim.

There is a common impression around, and certainly among many children, that pilgrimages are odd and exotic and this view is reinforced by stories of medieval extravagencies like climbing steps upon the knees. Those who have been on a pilgrimage are usually more impressed by the normality and ordinariness of it all. This point is made by the following account written by a rather articulate 12-year old girl of a pilgrimage she made to the English shrine of Our Lady of Walsingham from her suburban Church of England parish. This conveys, one suspects, the atmosphere of a fairly typical modern pilgrimage. (*Note about Walsingham*: Walsingham is a small village in the county of Norfolk which houses the restored shrine of Our Lady. In 1061 Richeldis, Lady of the Manor of Walsingham, received three visions of Mary in which she was shown the Holy House in Nazareth where Jesus had grown up. She was particularly told to note the dimensions so that she could build a replica. Richeldis did this and also built a church to cover the Holy House. So Walsingham, England's Nazareth, became a shrine of international patronage until the Reformation when it was destroyed and the Virgin's image burnt at Smithfield. In 1931 the Vicar of the parish began the process of restoring the shrine. The Roman Catholic Church acquired the Slipper Chapel in 1934, the place where pilgrims remove their shoes to walk the last mile. About half a million pilgrims now visit Walsingham each year.)

> The coach was due outside the church on Saturday morning at 8.00 am to take us to Walsingham. At five to eight all but two of us were there because Father Alan said that the coach was going to leave on time and anybody who missed it

An Extended Topic: Pilgrimage

would be left behind and not get a refund. In the end the only person late was Father Alan and we couldn't go without him because he was leading the pilgrimage. I went with my mum. My dad didn't want to go so he stayed at home to look after Andrew and Paul. On the coach I sat with my friend, Carol, who is 13. We stopped at Newmarket at a hotel with a nice garden. We sat in the sunshine and had sandwiches and a drink. Carol and I had cokes and lots of others had beer. Father Alan had gin. When we left the hotel the coach driver said that the next stop was Walsingham.

I had not been to Walsingham before but my mum had and she thought it was nice. Father Alan had told us about the story of the Virgin Mary appearing to a lady called Richeldis in 1061 and telling her to build a copy of Jesus' home in Nazareth. My friend Carol asked Father Alan if it was true. He said he didn't know but whether it was or not Walsingham was a very special place because so many people had been there to pray.

As we got near to Walsingham some people began to sing a long song which told the story of Walsingham right from the start. About a mile from Walsingham we stopped at a place called the Slipper Chapel which was where in olden days pilgrims used to take off their shoes and walk the last mile with bare feet. Some from our church wanted to walk the last mile. Carol and I were a bit stiff from sitting so we decided to walk too but we kept our shoes on.

Walsingham was really lovely. It was very pretty but it wasn't just that. It was sort of still and deep as well. We all met up with Father Alan and the coach outside the church. Father Alan was a bit cross because he thought the walkers had taken their time. We all went into the shrine and said some prayers by an altar near the door. Father Alan said we could have five minutes in the shrine church before we had to go to find out where we were to sleep. The shrine was lovely. It was quite dark and there were golden altars everywhere. Inside the church was a much smaller building and my mum said this was a copy of Mary's house at Nazareth. We went inside this. It was quite small and would have been very dark except that hundreds of candles were burning in it. They made it very hot. At the other end was an altar and above it was a statue of Mary wearing a golden robe holding the baby Jesus in her left arm and a large lily in her right arm. It made me feel quite excited.

Then we had to go to find out where we were to sleep. Carol and I were lucky as we were sharing a room in the convent. Mr. and Mrs. Pink had to sleep out in the village and weren't very pleased. We had supper and in the evening there was a procession outside round the shrine grounds. Four men, all from our parish, carried a statue of Our Lady of Walsingham, and the rest of us — and there were lots of people — carried candles and sang the hymn we had sung in the coach. A man took photographs of us as we walked. After this Carol and I had to go to bed. All the grown-ups seemed to go out. In the morning my mum told me that they had all gone down to the pub for a drink and played snooker. Father Alan surprised them all by being really good at snooker.

Early Sunday morning each parish had its own eucharist in different parts of the shrine church. We were lucky because we were given the Holy House for our service. After breakfast Father Alan was doing Stations of the Cross. All round the gardens there were pictures of Jesus on his way to his crucifixion. On the way he stopped fourteen times and there was a picture for each one. Father Alan took us from one to the next and stopped to say a prayer before each one.

After that we were free and Carol and I went for a walk round Walsingham. It was really lovely. We found a funny old railway station with the door open. We went inside and it was a church but different. We asked Father Alan and he told us that it was Russian Orthodox.

In the afternoon, Carol and I were walking with our mums down the main street going to look at the photographs the man had taken the night before when a fleet of coaches, full of West Indians, arrived. They all climbed out and began to process to the Slipper Chapel. They were led by a steel band and everyone was singing and dancing and clapping. It was really happy and you couldn't help joining in. Father Alan told us that they were Roman Catholics and that they kept the Slipper Chapel as their shrine.

Before we left, there was another procession — of Christ in His Blessed Sacrament. Some boys from our parish helped with this. This made Carol ever so cross because she felt it wasn't fair that boys could do all these things but girls never had the chance. It didn't worry me because I was happy just to watch. Just before the coach went I had the chance to go by myself into the Holy House. This was the loveliest bit and I said a prayer for my grandad who was ill.

An Extended Topic: Pilgrimage

At five o'clock prompt the coach left and we were on our way home. I liked Walsingham. It is a very special place. I want to go again soon.

This account conveys something of the pilgrim's feelings — of atmosphere, of 'specialness', of awe and devotion. It portrays pilgrimages, too, as a group activity — pilgrimages are rarely solitary — with all that entails in terms of togetherness and bonhomie. It presents too the idea of pilgrimages as an interweaving of religious feeling with the rest of life: the pilgrimage weekend to Walsingham contained both moments of deep and tender devotion and also playing snooker in the pub and grumbling about lodgings! This is a long way from many people's idea of pilgrimages as humourless and unsmiling affairs.

Pilgrimages in the Classroom

Any work on pilgrimages in the classroom should attempt to move beyond the level of information, for example, of learning what a Muslim does on the Hajj, important though that is, though this will of course at the factual level, be the starting point.

The following aims should point the work in the right direction:

(i) to help children to know something of pilgrimages made in different religions;
(ii) to help children to develop some awareness of why people go on pilgrimage;
(iii) to help children to begin to see life as a pilgrimage/journey in search of meaning.

On approaching the work it is likely that *explicit* work on pilgrimages will start with children who are 10 years old or more. Before that foundation work is likely to be provided by a general topic on 'journeys'.

Journeys

Journeys is a popular topic with younger children because it arises so naturally from their own experiences and can be developed in so many different ways:

(i) How we came to school this morning.
(ii) What roads did we go down?
(iii) How did we come — on foot, by car?

(iv) Did we come on our own, with friends?
(v) Journeys on holiday — by car, coach, train, aeroplane, boat.
(vi) Difficult journeys — being stuck in the snow, breaking down in the car.
(vii) Frightening journeys — crossing a rough sea, driving over a high bridge or viaduct ('I kept my eyes shut tight!').
(viii) Exciting journeys — into space, climbing up hills and mountains.
(ix) Boring journeys.
(x) Imaginary journeys — journeys I would like to make.
(xi) Good places to arrive at — grandparents, holiday centre, a fun fair. It is very easy to see how this can extend language work and develop mathematics, early map work and a host of things. It can also extend into other areas of study such as transport and into related areas such as the journey of a letter.

As far as religious education is concerned, there may be explicit material. For example, if this topic was being followed close to Christmas, then it might be appropriate to include the terrible journey that Mary had to make, according to the Nativity stories in St. Luke's Gospel, from Nazareth to Bethlehem. Certainly the children's work on difficult journeys and frightening journeys would give them a much more human understanding of it. Seen as preliminary work on pilgrimages the content of 'journeys' is much more likely to be implicit. It would be concerned to focus upon encouraging the children to reflect upon their *experiences* of journeys: of the excitement of anticipation, of the pleasure of arrival and of some of the hazards which occur on the way.

Approaches to Pilgrimage

With children of 10 years of age or more, the teacher can plan work much more specifically geared to pilgrimage and reflecting the aims which have been identified.

Because the teacher is very concerned to develop the children's *affective* understanding of the activities as well as a cognitive understanding, an approach through literature can be very helpful. This would be an example of *implicit* Religious education, but RE none the less.

An Extended Topic: Pilgrimage

Through literature

An approach which many teachers have found successful is that of studying books which deal with the notion of an individual's or a group's search or quest of something which is of great importance to them. This in itself will not meet the first aim of providing knowledge about pilgrimages like that to Lourdes. It is more concerned to deal with the third aim of helping children to begin to see life as a pilgrimage in search of meaning.

What follows consists of detailed discussions of two useful books and some comments of reservation on a third.

Ninny's Boat, by Clive King, published by Kestrel Books (1980) and Puffin Books (1983)
Ninny's Boat is set in Europe in the fifth century AD. Ninny, a slave boy in the land of the Angles (modern Denmark), is the property of an unpleasant owner, Sprott, who works him hard. So distrustful is he of people — they laugh at his name and at his small dark appearance — that he opts for the company of his animals, his true friends. He knows nothing of his true friends. He knows nothing of his origins or his age with the exception of a recurring bad dream — a dream in which there is darkness and the sound of women screaming and he, a tiny child, is wrapped in a blanket in the dark and the rain — and then there is the heaving of waves ...

One morning Ninny awakes in his hay loft in Anglia to find himself isolated in the middle of a great flood. The others have fled, forgetting him, so he sets about rescuing himself and his animals from drowning. He finds safety on a larger island in the flood waters and, after initially an unpleasant reception by the people there, he begins to find friendship and respect and to be regarded as an equal. When the elders ponder how they might escape, it is Ninny who suggests that they build a boat. When the boat is being built, Ninny plays an important part in the process. When the boat sets sail for the Isles of the Ocean, Ninny also travels in it, taking his precious animals. After a terrifying journey across the seas, it is Ninny who steers the boat in a storm over the sand bar which brings the people safely to Britannia, the Isle of the Ocean.

Here Ninny finds that people do not laugh at his name and that there are others who resemble him physically. He begins his search in a long journey up the centre of Britannia, through the mountains and moors, to the Great Wall and then to the sea. He is caught up innocently in a great and terrible battle and, in ferrying the dying king in a boat with two black clad women, he reaches a white building in a rocky bay — all of which he has dreamed before.

It is in this building, a Christian monastery, that Ninny learns who he is. He is no longer Ninny, but Ninian, named in honour of the great Celtic Saint, and the kidnapped son of King Urr, a prince but without a kingdom.

The story is full of symbolism of pilgrimage and journey. The flight from the flood and the building of the boat evoke the story of Noah and his Ark. There are also very clear allusions to the Arthurian legends. It is not specially for this reason that a teacher may want to use the book in the context of a study of pilgrimage. Above all the story is of a physical journey which both parallels and facilitates Ninny's own journey of self discovery.

I Am David by Anne Holm published by Methuen (1965) and Puffin (1969)

I Am David, perhaps because it was written some years before is much better known in schools than *Ninny's Boat*. *I Am David* also uses the device of using a physical journey to mirror a spiritual journey.

I Am David, set in this century, but without any clear location, is the story of a boy who escapes from the concentration camp in which he has been reared with the instruction to travel north until he comes to Denmark. He knows nothing of his parents or of his origin: only that he is David. In the camp he had one friend, a man Johannes who was like a father to him but who died. It was Johannes who taught him all he knew. For all other humans, David felt suspicion and hatred. His journey to Denmark is full of adventure and hazard but out of these experiences David begins to make discoveries for himself, slowly and suspiciously! He begins to discover an appreciation of beauty, of laughter, of love and affection and of freedom. The story is of David's journey to Denmark but embedded in it are the experiences which help him to see who he, David, really is. It ends in Denmark where David finds his mother and so also his roots and the place where he belongs.

This is the real value of the book to the theme of pilgrimage: presenting life as a search for meaning, as a continuous journey. There are specific incidents in the book which could be seen as either directly religious or of being close parallels. David prays to 'the God of the green pastures and still waters'; one of his earliest actions after escape was to wash his clothes and his body until they were thoroughly clean; a sheepdog which attached itself to David is shot so that he can escape. There is a natural tendency for a teacher, especially one

An Extended Topic: Pilgrimage

looking at the book from a specifically religious angle, to develop these: the meaning of faith, the parallels with Baptism and with Crucifixion. These temptations should be resisted, unless they arise naturally. In this context, the reason for using the book is to encourage the children to reflect upon David's personal journey of discover.

Another book which could be used in this context is:

The Silver Sword by Ian Seraillier published by Jonathan Cape/Puffin Books. Like *I Am David* this is well-known to children. Set in war time Poland, it tells of three children who are separated from their parents. After surviving the war they set out with a friend on the seemingly impossible tasks of finding their parents in the haystack of Europe.

The Pilgrim's Progress by John Bunyan
Although it is among the best known books in the English language, few today have read it and certainly in its adult form it is not suitable for use with children of the age we are considering. A useful re-telling of the story can be found in James Reeves *Quest and Conquest* published by Blackie in 1976.

Bunyan was a Puritan in the seventeenth century and his book is an allegory of the spiritual journey of the Christian or perhaps more precisely the spiritual journey as understood by puritan theology. The hero of the work, Christian, leaves his home in the City of Destruction to journey to the Celestial City. On the way many things happen to him: he falls into the Slough of Despond, he meets Mr. Worldly Wiseman, he falls into the hands of Giant Despair and is imprisoned in Doubting Castle; he is subjected to the cruelty of Vanity Fair and much much else. Finally in the end he reaches the Celestial City.

At one level, it is a splendid story. Any adult too can see that the names of the characters and the places point to another level of meaning. Now children of 12 years or so can be helped to see this through imaginative discussion. Christian fell into the Slough of Despond. What did this mean? Do they have anything in their own experience which illuminates it? The same could be done in a discussion about Doubting Castle and Giant Despair. Having said this, many teachers find that this is as far as they can go! *Parts* of the book are fascinating to children and they can respond to them, but what of others such as the great pack which Christian carried on his back. This is a much more difficult and remote notion. Beyond all this is the consideration that the *Pilgrim's Progress* deals with a type of interior pilgrimage which is remote to the experience of all but a very few today. It is unlikely that many children in the secularized societies of

Western Europe will find much rapport with Christian's pilgrimage *per se*. Neither will many others nurtured in other Christian traditions which would not see the Christian's spiritual pilgrimage in those terms. The experience of many teachers is that this is not in the end a very helpful book for this purpose at this age.

Pilgrimages in World Religions

The aims would be the same three as those listed at the beginning of the section:

(i) to help children to know something of pilgrimages made in different religions;
(ii) to help children to develop some awareness of why people go on pilgrimage;
(iii) to help children to begin to see life as a pilgrimage journey in search of meaning.

In this approach the religious material will be explicit.

A possible approach:

(i) a discussion of secular parallels to religious pilgrimage, emphasizing sharing enthusiasm, fellow feeling and common purpose, for example, pop concerts and festivals, political marches, special sports games;
(ii) an introduction of a medieval pilgrimage such as the one to Canterbury described by Chaucer emphasizing the mixed nature of many of the pilgrims but the religious nature of the journey for many of the pilgrims;
(iii) the idea of special places, sacred to different religions, for example, Jerusalem for Jews, Christians and Moslems, Mecca for Moslems, Lourdes and Walsingham for Christians and so on.
(iv) Case Study I: Jerusalem
   (a) Western ('Wailing') Wall of the Temple for Jews.
   (b) Via Dolorosa (Christ's final journey) for Christians.
   (c) Dome of the Rock for Moslems.
   Finding why these places are sacred.
(v) Case Study II: The Hajj
   What happens on the Hajj? Why is it so special?
(vi) Case study III: Lourdes
   What made Lourdes into a special place of pilgrimage? What happens there today?

9 Christian Festivals

Like all religions Christianity has many holy days in the course of the year. Of these the most special tend to focus upon events in the life of Jesus Christ. The two principal feasts are Christmas and Easter, both of which have before them a period of preparation (Advent and Lent). There are also many festivals associated with saints, that is, exceptional followers of Christ. It should be noted though that there are some traditions within Christianity in which festivals hold comparatively little significance for adherents. In this account what is described relates to what is found in the life of the more ancient and numerically strongest churches of Christendom.

The aim of this chapter is to give some basic information about the festivals and fasts of the Christian year which can be used as a factual starting point for both classroom teaching and for stories told in assembly. Where it is appropriate, relevant passages from the Bible are given. Chapter 10 will look in some detail at the teaching of festivals in the primary classroom, bearing in mind the different ages and stages of the children.

Advent

Advent marks the beginning of the Christian year and is a period of around four weeks immediately prior to Christmas. It is seen by Christians as a time of preparation and penitence. The message through the Bible readings and the Advent hymns and carols is summed up by the word 'awake'. Worshippers begin to prepare for the coming of Jesus both as the baby born at Bethlehem and as Judge of both the individual and the world. The appearance of churches tends to be sober in order to reflect this mood. Altar cloths and vestments tend to be violet or purple in colour and flowers are removed.

Religious Education 5–12

Two traditional customs which emphasize the nature of Advent as a period of preparation are the use of both the Advent calendar and the Advent corona. With the Advent calendar, the user opens a small numbered door or window on each day of the Advent season. Each one reveals a different picture culminating, on the final day, with a representation of the Nativity. With the Advent corona one candle is lit on each Sunday of the Advent season.

Christmas (25 December)

Perhaps the most popular festival of the Christian faith, at least in the western church, Christmas celebrates the birth of Christ in Bethlehem. Beneath this it is really celebrating the Incarnation, the entry of God into humanity. The well known Christmas stories are recorded in St. Matthew, chapter 1, verses 18–25 and St. Luke, chapter 2, verses 1–20 and concern the census, the birth in the stable and the visit by the shepherds. A reflection on the significance of the events is given in St. John, chapter 1, verses 1–14.

Churches tend to be richly decorated with flowers, the Advent colours are replaced with whites and golds and many churches are ablaze with candles, symbolizing the entry of the Light into the world. An extremely popular service is the Midnight Mass. Many churches also erect a crib, depicting the scene in the stable with Mary, Joseph and the Shepherds. The figures of Father Christmas or Santa Claus arise from St. Nicholas, patron saint of children who traditionally brought them gifts of toys on his own feast day in December.

Epiphany (6 January)

Also called Twelfth Night, Epiphany ends the Christmas season: hence the old tradition of clearing away all the Christmas decorations by this date. Epiphany means (literally) 'manifestation' and it is associated with the manifestation or showing forth of the infant Christ to the Gentiles, in the figures of the wise men or magi who followed the star.

The story is told in Matthew, chapter 2, verses 1–12. In the popular mind it is elided with Christmas but in the church's year it is used to emphasise this universal aspect of the coming of Christ. Many churches which have cribs will remove the shepherds and replace them with images of the magi bearing their symbolic gifts of gold, frankincense and myrrh. Hymns associated with this festival are *We Three Kings of Orient Are* and *Bethlehem of Noblest Cities*.

Candlemas (2 February)

Candlemas is the abbreviated way of describing the feast otherwise known as 'The Purification of the Blessed Virgin Mary' or 'The Presentation of Christ in the Temple'. This commemorates the incident when Mary and Joseph in observation of the law brought the infant Jesus to the temple to present him to God and make a thank offering. While in the temple, two old and devout Jews, Simeon and Anna recognized the specialness of Jesus and Simeon spoke the famous hymn, the Nunc Dimittis. In this he hailed Christ as the 'light to lighten the Gentiles and the glory of thy people, Israel'. The story is found in Luke, chapter 2, verses 22–35. It is this theme of Christ who will bring the light of the knowledge of God to the whole world which is emphasized and in its full form the Candlemas ceremonies include a procession of the whole congregation around the church carrying lighted candles.

Lady Day (25 March)

More fully entitled 'The Annunciation of Our Lord to the Blessed Virgin Mary', this feast celebrates the announcement of the future birth of Christ. According to the account in Luke, chapter 1, verses 26–38, the angel Gabriel comes to Mary, a young engaged woman in Nazareth and announces that she has been chosen to bear a son, Jesus, through the operation of the Holy Spirit. The account concludes with Mary's acceptance: 'Behold the handmaid of the Lord; be it unto me according to thy word'. This is a popular festival, especially among women.

Lent

As Advent is the period of preparation for Christmas, so Lent is for Easter. It is also longer, lasting forty days, and is more widely observed. It is a period of penitence in which the faithful attempt to work harder at their religion. Three key ideas of Lent are prayer, almsgiving and fasting. So in Lent Christians try to spend more time in prayer and study, often reading more of their Bibles or studying a religious book either singly or in groups. There is an effort too to think more of others and this self-denial underlies both almsgiving and fasting. This is the background to the old custom of giving up something luxurious that one enjoys for Lent and then giving the money saved to charity. Fasting, as well as being a form of self-denial, is also a way of bringing the body under the control of the spirit! In the early centuries the Lenten fast was very strict, only one meal a day was allowed and no meat or fish. This has gradually been relaxed and now in, for example, the Roman Catholic Church, only Ash Wednesday and Good Friday are fast days in this sense.

Churches also express the same note of penitence and self-denial. The hangings and vestments are purple or violet and as Good Friday approaches crucifixes and statues are often veiled.

Ash Wednesday

The first day of Lent, and a solemn day, Ash Wednesday is intended to be kept as a day of fasting. Its name comes from the ancient and widespread practice of ashing. At the beginning of the Ash Wednesday eucharist worshippers come forward to have a cross marked with ash on their foreheads. As the priest places the mark there he speaks the words, 'Remember, O man, that dust thou art and unto dust shalt thou return'. This is intended to set the mood for Lent.

The day immediately prior to Ash Wednesday is *Shrove Tuesday*. This term comes from the old verb 'to shrive' (to confess) when the faithful made their confessions and were given absolution. Today it is better known for its pancakes and its pancake races. This tradition comes from the custom of eating up all the food in the house which would be forbidden in Lent.

Mothering Sunday

Mid-Lent Sunday or the Fourth Sunday in Lent has traditionally been called Mothering Sunday. The probable reason for this is that it was the day when children who had left home returned to visit their mothers. Traditionally they would bring with them bunches of flowers and sometimes a simnel cake. This custom is continued in many churches and children come up during the service to receive little bunches of flowers which they give to their mothers. It is also called

Refreshment Sunday, probably because the day was a relaxation in the self-denial of Lent.

Holy Week

Holy Week is the week stretching from Palm Sunday and Easter Day which includes Maundy Thursday, Good Friday and Holy Saturday.

Palm Sunday

Palm Sunday commemorates the entry of Christ into Jerusalem on a donkey to the acclamation of the crowds who placed palm leaves and garments in his path. Christ enters the city and then goes to the temple (Mark, chapter 11, verses 1–11). The symbolism for Christians is that here Christ is entering the holy city and its temple as King. The day is marked by the blessing and distribution of palms (small crosses made out of palm leaves) and there is usually a procession of both priest and people to the singing of a hymn, often *All Glory, Laud and Honour to Thee Redeemer King*. In some parishes, a donkey, where one is available, is added to the procession. It is a bitter-sweet occasion because although the service begins with this joyful procession it later contains a long reading of the Passion and Death of Christ.

Maundy Thursday

This is the Thursday before Easter when Christ met in the upper room with his disciples for the Last Supper (Mark chapter 14, verses 12–31, John, chapter 13, verses 1–15). This was the occasion of the Institution of the Eucharist, when Jesus blessed and broke bread. Jesus also washed his disciples' feet as an example of how they ought to treat each other. After the meal, Jesus and the disciples went to the Garden of Gethsemane (Mark, chapter 14, verses 32–52). Here Jesus endured a period of mental agony during which his disciples slept. Judas then betrayed Jesus to the soldiers, he was arrested and led away.

On Maundy Thursday, worshippers are torn between giving thanks for the Eucharist and being aware of the awful context in which it is taking place. For this reason the main focus for thanksgiving for the Eucharist tends to be the Feast of Corpus Christi in early summer.

In many churches a feature of the services is the washing of feet, following in the example of Christ. Each year, for example, the Pope washes the feet of beggars in St. Peter's, Rome. The English custom of the Sovereign distributing Maundy money is a survival of the ancient footwashing. Originally the Sovereign did wash the feet of beggars but this was transposed into the giving of money.

After the end of the Eucharist, it is very common for churches to be stripped of hangings, cloths, crosses and so on to make them as bare as possible to symbolize the deriliction of Good Friday. In many churches too a small altar is prepared covered with flowers, called the Altar of Repose. This symbolizes the Garden of Gethsemane and worshippers can watch with Christ in his agony.

Good Friday

Good Friday is so called only because its effects are good for the world. It commemorates the crucifixion of Jesus, his death and hurried burial. It is the most solemn day of the Christian year. It is recorded in all four gospels, each of which give it their own emphasis: Matthew, chapter 27, verses 24–66, Mark, chapter 15, verses 15–47, Luke, chapter 23, verses 26–56, John, chapter 19, verses 1–42. Churches are bare of any ornament from the stripping of the previous evening. For the Christian, it is a most unpleasant day. It is observed in a variety of ways. Many churches offer a Three Hours' Devotion, timed from 12.00 noon to 3.00 pm, the last three hours on the cross, which is a series of devotional addresses interspersed with hymns. Others abbreviate this to one hour. Others celebrate the liturgy for the day which includes acts of devotion to the cross of Christ. Pilgrims in Jerusalem will follow the traditional path which Jesus took on his way from his condemnation to Golgotha. According to tradition he stopped fourteen times on this journey, the Via Dolorosa (The Way of Sorrow) and each spot is marked. These are called the Stations of the Cross and many churches go through these using representations and pictures.

A traditional custom on Good Friday is eating hot cross buns.

Easter Eve

Easter Eve, the Saturday between Good Friday and Easter Sunday, is the one complete day in which Jesus lay in the tomb. In practice churches cannot be left as they were on Good Friday because it takes time to decorate them with flowers and greenery for the splendour of Easter Day.

In the evening of the day it is traditional for the Easter Eve Vigil to be held. This begins with the kindling of the new fire, usually a small bonfire outside the church, which symbolizes the new light, life and energy of the Resurrection of Jesus. From this fire the great Pascal (Easter) candle is lit and carried into the dark church. Three times the deacon who is carrying the candle sings: *The Light of Christ* and each time the people reply *Thanks Be to God*. Then is sung the *Exultet* which lays out the significance of the night and why it is the reason for universal joy. Then there are nine readings and a sermon. The congregation then moves to the font for the blessing of the baptismal waters and any who have been prepared for baptism are baptised at this point. The whole congregation then renews its own baptismal vows. After this there is normally the first Eucharist of Easter. This is particularly significant among the Orthodox Churches of the East.

Easter Day

Easter Day is the celebration of the Resurrection of Christ from the dead and for the new life which is promised to his people. It is the oldest and the greatest of all Christian festivals. Churches are usually decked with flowers and it is traditional for arum lilies to be in evidence. Many churches have Easter gardens which depict the three empty crosses and the empty tomb with the folded grave clothes.

The accounts of the Resurrection are found in all four gospels Matthew, chapter 28, verses 1–20, Mark, chapter 16, verses 1–20, Luke, chapter 24, verses 1–49, and John, chapters 20 and 21. All accounts are agreed that (i) on the Sunday the stone covering the mouth of the tomb had been rolled back and that not only was the tomb empty but also that the grave clothes were neatly folded; (ii) that the disciples were not expecting to find the tomb empty; and (iii) that the disciples met with Jesus. Particularly memorable stories are the two disciples walking to Emmaus who met with Jesus along the way but only recognized him in the breaking of bread (Luke, chapter 24, verses 13–35) and the story of Mary Magdalene weeping by the tomb and finding that the man she had supposed to be the gardener was Jesus (John, chapter 20, verses 11–18).

It is an old custom to give eggs at Easter — often chocolate ones. In some parts eggs are hard boiled, dyed and decorated and sometimes these are rolled down hills. Sometimes the symbolism is in the rolling away of the stone from the mouth of the tomb. Usually, though, the symbolism is one of new life: out of the hard, lifeless egg bursts forth the fresh new life of the chick.

The date of Easter Day varies from year to year, though it always falls within the limits of 21 March and 25 April. This is because its date is determined by the date of the Jewish feast of Passover and that in turn is determined by the moon.

Ascension Day

Ascension Day celebrates the end of Christ's resurrection appearances and his exaltation into heaven. According to Acts chapter 1, verse 3, it happened forty days after Easter. An account is given in Acts, chapter 1, verses 3–9. Theologically it is regarded as the feast of the Lordship of Christ over all creation.

Whitsunday (Pentecost)

This is celebrated as the birthday of the church. The account is found in the Acts of the Apostles, chapter 2, verses 1–4 when the Holy Spirit came upon the church. It is central to the Christian faith that the church is guided, inspired and sustained by the Spirit of God. The real name of the feast is Pentecost but it is commonly known as Whitsunday. It falls fifty days after Easter.

Harvest

An unofficial but very popular festival, especially strong in Britain, giving thanks for the fruits of the earth. It is usually held on a Sunday in September or October after the harvest has been gathered. It may be associated with a parish harvest supper. People bring along fruit or vegetables and the church is decorated with these. In some urban industrial areas, harvest festivals have included items made in factories and workshops in the area.

All Saints and All Souls (1 and 2 November)

All Saints' Day celebrates and gives thanks for the lives of all Christian saints (that is, Christians who have been 'lights of the world in their

Christian Festivals

several generations') known and unknown. It is also, less commonly, called *All Hallows Day*. With it is associated *Halloween* (the Eve of All Hallows) on 31 October. The notion was that the celebration of so much goodness on All Saints' Day naturally brought out all the forces of evil, and as forces of evil are associated with darkness, so the night before All Saints was full of the symbols of evil — witches, wizards, sprites, goblins, ghosts and so on. With the dawn of All Saints Day, the goodness and the light drove them from the scene. Once a time of real fear, Halloween is now a party time with children (and adults) dressing up as witches and wizards.

All Souls' Day follows All Saints' and brings to mind all the dead. At the requiem on that day, long lists of names of departed members of churches and of families are read out and prayers are offered for their rest. In some countries it is the custom at this season for people to light lamps on the graves of their departed members.

Throughout the year, special saints have their own days. Here is a list of some of the most prominent.

25 January	St. Paul (Acts, chapter 9, verses 1–22)
19 March	St. Joseph, husband of the Blessed Virgin Mary (Matthew, chapter 1, verses 18–25)
11 June	St. Barnabas (Acts, chapter 11, verses 19–30)
29 June	St. Peter (Mark, chapter 8, verses 27–30)
22 July	St. Mary Magdalene (John, chapter 20, verses 11–18)
25 July	St. James the Apostle (Mark, chapter 10, verses 35–45)
21 September	St. Matthew the Apostle (Matthew, chapter 9, verses 9–13)
30 November	St. Andrew (Matthew, chapter 4, verses 12–20)

Other saints popular among children are:

1 March	St. David, patron of Wales
17 March	St. Patrick, patron of Ireland
23 April	St. George, patron of England
26 May	St. Augustine of Canterbury
27 May	Venerable Bede
22 June	St. Alban, the first British martyr
4 October	St. Francis of Assisi

10 Teaching Festivals

Festivals are a feature of all religions and appeal to worshippers of all ages. By their very nature they are community affairs (social dimension) and they re-enact in a familiar way (ritual dimension) aspects of the religion which are significant to believers. In addition to this they inevitably both reflect and point to central beliefs of the religion, though the understanding possessed by worshippers may be at different levels. A case in point is Christmas. Christians celebrate Christmas together, performing certain rituals including the singing of special hymns or carols. Christmas for Christians reflects and points to the centre of Christian belief, the Incarnation, but the festival can be understood by different believers at different levels ranging from a thanksgiving for a special baby to a thanksgiving for the Incarnation of God in humanity. Festivals are an important means of enabling believers to work their way both emotionally and intellectually into the heart of their religion.

In this section there will be a consideration of some approaches to teaching about a number of Christian festivals but before this there are some important foundations to lay in the infant years.

Foundation Work on Festivals

Before a teacher does specific work on any one festival with children, it is important to examine the underlying notion of *special days*. Children can learn facts about different festivals but if they are to understand what believers feel about them then they must see them in the same way as they see festivals (special days) in their own lives — like birthdays. Again, children can study birthday customs of children in other parts of the world and this can be both interesting and impersonal. When they realize that, involved with these customs are the same feelings of anticipation, excitement and joy which they feel on their own birthdays then the whole exercise takes on a new depth of meaning. So it is with festivals. Festivals can be very interesting things to study but they can be amazingly impersonal (for example, 'On Palm Sunday, people in church carry palm crosses ...'). They take on a new depth of meaning when the person studying festivals suddenly realizes that participants feel about these occasions as they feel about their own special days.

It is therefore very important that young children should be encouraged to focus on *'celebrating'*.

A Possible Approach

Aims

To encourage children:

(i) to think about their special or happy days;
(ii) to acknowledge the rituals which happen on these days;
(iii) to recognize and to begin to articulate the emotions associated with these occasions.

Focus upon 'my birthday' because it:

(i) is highly significant in the lives of most individuals;
(ii) has widespread and time hallowed rituals associated with it;
(iii) is one of the closest experiences to a religious festival.

Possible development

Teachers will wish to develop the idea in a variety of ways, through talk, pictures, stories, simple writing, drama, music and so on.

The following are points of focus arising from a consideration of a fairly common pattern of a child's birthday in this country:

waking up and being given the first cards and presents;
waiting (impatiently) at the window for the postman to come;
opening cards and presents, special wrapping paper, difficult string;

preparing for the party:

the smell of cakes being baked, sandwiches being made;

preparing for party games — wrapping up the parcel for Pass the Parcel;
laying the table; putting out the names by each place; who is going to sit by me?;
getting washed and dressed in party clothes;

the party:

waiting for the doorbell to ring;
opening the door; the bustle; the presents; not enough time to open them;
being the centre of attention;
playing the party games — passing the parcel, musical chairs, musical statues, sticking the tail on the donkey;
having tea; special cake; candles, one for each year of age;
the singing of Happy Birthday;
blowing out the candles;
packing up the cake in napkins to take home;
goodbye, tiredness and bed.

Another focus under 'celebrating' could be my cousin's wedding

The aims would be the same as with 'my birthday' and teachers would approach it in the same way. Possible focusses are:

being a bridesmaid/page boy;
special clothes: white dress, veils, bridesmaids in long dresses;
'something old, something new, something borrowed, something blue';
special flowers — bouquets, flowers in church;
special buildings: church, registry office;
special people: clergy, registrars;
special words, including promises;
special music;
confetti, rice, messages on cars;
the reception — eating, drinking, dancing.

Christmas

Preliminary Considerations

1 This is the most popular festival of the year, at least in Western Christendom. It will therefore, be celebrated in each of

Teaching Festivals

the seven or eight years during which the child is in primary school. Great care is needed not to evoke the reaction 'not again' with the 11-year-olds!

2 It is possible to understand the significance of Christmas at different levels and it is important not to rush children's understanding. It is better to get them *pointed in the right direction*.

3 Like most festivals Christmas has many themes within it (for example: babies, gifts, light in darkness). It is often best to focus on just one of these on a given occasion and some are, of course, more suited to different age groups.

4 It is possible to 'understand' Christmas on an emotional as well as an intellectual level.

Below are some possible approaches to teaching about Christmas, directed towards different age groups.

With Infants

The adult understanding of Christmas as the Feast of the Incarnation is clearly beyond young children. It is obviously best to concentrate upon the *emotional feel* of Christmas rather than the intellectual understanding.

The 'feel' of Christmas

Aims

(i) To examine the different elements of Christmas.
(ii) To enrich and enhance the associated feelings of joy, excitement and wonder.

Most people know the feeling of Christmas. The excitement which gradually builds up: only ten shopping days to Christmas! Children share this too and can be helped to see more into the significance of Christmas.

Children will find in the celebration of Christmas a number of elements: holly, ivy, mistletoe, Christmas trees, paper decorations, candles, yule logs. Father Christmas, cards, presents, nativity scenes, carols in frosty air, cribs, roast turkey, plum pudding, cake and so on. These elements are from different sources by no means all Christian, but together they make up the emotional feel of Christmas. To enrich the child's existing joy, excitement and wonder is both a very important foundation for a developing appreciation of Christmas and also a realistic and reasonable approach at the level of the child.

Birthdays

Aims

(i) To tell the story of the birth of Jesus in the stable.
(ii) To focus upon the sort of birthday Jesus as a child might have enjoyed.

Christmas celebrates the birthday of Jesus and a birthday is a point of contact with young children.

Introduce the birth of Jesus in the stable, bringing out the themes of absence from home, the inns being full, and the warm welcoming straw.

What sort of things happened at birthdays in the time of Jesus? What sort of games did children play? A number of teachers have looked at the birthday of Jesus when he was 5 or 6-years-old.

Babies

Aims

(i) To discuss the sorts of things involved in preparing for the coming of a baby today.
(ii) Against that background to tell the story of Mary's journey and the birth of Jesus in the stable.

A popular approach with many infants' teachers is 'Babies', especially if any of the class is expecting a brother or sister. One particular teacher did a very successful strand of work over a six-week period in which the class followed the preparations of one of the mothers for her expected child: refurbishing the pram, repainting the cot, scrubbing the car seat and so on. All this made the story of Mary's preparation seem much more like real life and her unexpected trip to Bethlehem at such a late stage quite horrifying!

With Juniors

Giving

Teaching Festivals

Aims

    (i)   Study the Nativity stories with a special focus upon those concerned with gifts.
    (ii) Discuss the reasons why people make gifts.
    (iii) Look at examples of people who have given a lot.
    (iv) Consider different ways in which all of us can give of ourselves.

A deep-rooted theme within the Nativity stories is that of 'giving'. The whole event is about the gift of Jesus to the world and within the stories there are two particular examples:

    (a) the Magi with their gifts of gold, frankincense and myrrh; and
    (b) the visit of the Shepherds to the manger bringing (according, at least, to tradition) a lamb.

These stories can be told and a discussion etc., can take place about gifts given and received. Focus upon the reasons for giving gifts: love, affection, thanks, concern, respect, regard and so on.

What sort of gifts have we to offer? health, strength, hands, feet, time, talents ...

Do some work on people who have been or are outstanding in their giving of themselves: for example, Jesus himself — stories of Jesus teaching, healing, helping and finally being executed.

Father Damien, the priest in the last century who volunteered to serve as priest on the leper island of Molokai in the Hawaian Islands. He worked tirelessly for the welfare of his lepers and eventually contracted the disease himself.

Mother Teresa who works among the sick and dying in Calcutta.

A consideration of ways in which all can give. For example, the work of Oxfam, Christian Aid, Shelter.

Effective ways of working within this theme, in addition to discussions and through the use of various types of writing, are through music, drama and art.

The Brotherhood of Man

Aims

    (i)   To discuss the significance of the Feast of the Epiphany.
    (ii) To consider the notion of the Family of God.

(iii) To investigate the implications within the idea of the Brotherhood of Man.

Tell the story of the Magi following the star. Make the point strongly that they were *non-Jews* and that the story was included to emphasize the fact that the gift of Jesus was for all people irrespective of race or creed. Refer to the Feast of the Epiphany (chapter 9) and to Candlemas (chapter 9) which makes a similar point.

Introduce the idea of the Family of God — that all people are children of God. Reference can be made to people like Martin Luther King and Ghandi who were motivated by such ideas.
Begin to examine the notion of the Family of God.
What are its implications? How does a family operate?
Concept of sharing, caring, protection, concern.
Begin to examine the kindred concept of the 'Brotherhood of Man'. What implications has this for treatment of fellow humans.
Role of agencies which work for the elimination of poverty.
Story of the Good Samaritan. (To whom am I neighbour?)
The strong notion of brotherhood in religions: in Christianity the notion of people being sons and daughters of God and the Church his Family; in Islam the strong notion of brotherhood which underlies the Hajj and Zakat.

Other approaches could be:

Family life in Palestine — What sort of home would Jesus have lived in? What sort of work did a carpenter do? What type of food would be prepared in the home? What sort of games did children play at the time.

Christmas: The Festival of Light — An important theme of Christmas is the entry of Christ as a light in the darkness. It can be very illuminative to explore with older juniors the symbolism of light. It can be linked with the Jewish festival of light, Chanukkah which falls in December. For further details see chapter 6.

11 The Bible

The Bible has always had an honoured place in religious education in a Christian environment or culture. In fact in British schools, certainly with children up to the age of 12 or 13, it used to form almost the total content of the religious education syllabus. A study of school syllabuses from the 1940s and 1950s shows this very clearly. In these it was often suggested to teachers that very young children should be given a selection of stories from the Bible under headings such as 'Stories Jesus told' (for example, the Parables) or 'Stories Jesus heard as a boy' (for example, stories from the Old Testament) and that when they reached the age of 7 or 8 years there should be more systematic treatment of the Bible, such as 'Abraham, Isaac, Jacob, Joseph, the Captivity in Egypt, Moses, the Exodus, the Promised Land' with the 7–8-year-olds, 'The Judges, Saul, David, Solomon, the division of the Kingdom' with the 8–9-year-olds and so on. The Bible was the text book of religious education and the aim of religious education lessons was to instill in children a knowledge of the Bible.

This central position of the Bible in religious education has been strongly challenged from two directions: firstly from the work done by Goldman and others (see chapter 3) investigating the development of children's religious concepts and secondly from the general movement away from a confessionalist approach in the teaching of religious education (see chapter 2).

It is argued in most recent syllabuses, following the lead given by Goldman, that the Bible is an adult book and therefore not suitable for young children. Moreover, the difficulties which children find with understanding much of the Bible are not problems of the *language* in which it is written but of the *concepts* within it. This means that a careful retelling of stories by the teacher in simple words does not really provide the answer. This in no way implies that young children should not be exposed to the Bible or that it should be kept under lock and key in dark stock cupboards! Rather it implies that teachers have to *select* carefully from it. A good image for the use of the Bible with young children is that of a quarry. There is a vast amount of valuable material there and teachers go to it to select pieces which are appropriate and useful for their purposes.

Selection implies a criterion and the essential one is *helpfulness*. Does this story from the Bible aid the development of children's religious understanding? Unless the teacher feels that the answer is a clear 'yes' then the story should not be used. We might define the development of religious understanding in this context as twofold: the gradual development of building up an accurate understanding of the Christian concept of God and secondly the developing of a mature understanding of what the Bible is. Is, for example, teaching 5-year-olds about 'the avenging angel of the Lord' or 6-year-olds the story of Abraham's attempted sacrifice of Isaac (Genesis, chapter 22, verses 1–13) helpful in the development of their religious understanding? Is the teacher laying helpful foundations or unhelpful ones?

One of the problems one faces is that the Old Testament particularly has many good stories: exciting, colourful, dramatic and often with an attractive touch of bloodthirstiness so it is not surprising that many figure strongly in young children's religious education — Joshua and the Battle of Jericho, the exploits of Samson and so on.

Noah's Ark, for example, has many qualities which make it attractive to teachers of young children. It has charm, it has colour, it has plenty of exciting repetition. It opens itself to drama and to a considerable amount of art work. Yet from the point of view of the development of young children's religious understanding there are two main areas of concern. Firstly, it could have implications for the child's image of God. The background to the story is that God is punishing the human race for its wickedness by the complete extermination of everyone except for Noah and his family. Children do perceive this ('I wouldn't do that to my rabbits' commented one 7-year-old!) so it does raise the question of what picture of God is being laid down in children's minds. Secondly, the story, because it is from the Bible, tends to be seen by the young child as true historically — even though the teacher may explain that it is not. The same child at 11 or 12 is inclined to perceive the historical improbability of the story and so to reject it as 'untrue' — and with it the whole Bible. Many secondary school teachers will find this situation only too familiar!

There has been some reaction in recent years to this position — what has been described as the 'religious veto'.[1] Some urge that we are

The Bible

too concerned with the young child's *conceptual* understanding of Bible stories. What is more important is *imaginative* understanding. We need to tell children the stories in order to feed and enrich their imaginations. It is often noted that in India children are raised on the stories of the gods from their earliest years. The stories enrich the children's religious imagination and no one much worries about their conceptual understanding. The role of the story — and in this context the religious story — is more to do with the affective than with the cognitive.

There are two points here which need careful thought:

(a) Children in a western culture are trained to assess things in terms of literal historical truth or falsity. We may not want them to approach these wonderful stories cognitively, but they will and they will also apply those considerations to biblical stories.

(b) There is perhaps an important difference between children raised in a believing setting to those who are not. The religious understanding of children reared in a religious home or well established in a worshipping community is much more likely to develop gradually and to move towards maturity than that of children without this setting. Positive attitudes towards religious ideas and ready help from sympathetic adults will foster the maturing process. Children without these influences are less likely to have such positive attitudes and are more likely to reject the Bible out of hand while they are still in an immature state of understanding. How many adults are there around who reject the Bible out of hand because they are still in the immature state of understanding in which they believe that the Bible presents the Creation stories in the Book of Genesis (chapters 1 and 2) as a scientific statement of how the universe came into being!?

The important point about the use of Bible stories with young children is that the teachers should ask themselves whether the story is helpful to the children in the long term development of their religious understanding or whether it will set up unhelpful attitudes or images. It is really a matter of professional judgment and over many stories teachers will disagree. Two teachers spent a whole lunchtime arguing about whether the story of the child Samuel in the Temple (1 Samuel, chapter 3, verses 1–10) was suitable for 8 and 9-year-olds and failed to come to an agreement! One took the view that it could be very distressing for young children to hear about a small boy being left by his mother and sleeping each night in a dark church. The other argued that the story is imbued with a considerable quality of religious awe and that this would feed children's imagination and that it also clearly illustrated the Judaeo Christian notion of the personal relationship between God and the individual.

Note

1 Priestley J. G. (1981) 'Religious story and the literary imagination', *British Journal of Religious Education*, 4, 1, Autumn; Nash P. (1983) 'A matter of integrity', *British Journal of Religious Education*, 5, 3, Summer

12 An Approach Through Bible Background

That Bible background has such a time-honoured place in religious education is a recognition that to many the Bible is a difficult book. This may be partly due to a lack of familiarity with it, to its traditional language (though there are, of course, many modern translations) or to a cultural difference between the twentieth century and the first century. An obvious example of this is the subjects of Jesus' parables. It is clear from the gospel records that Jesus was a powerful and authoritative story teller. Part of the appeal was the fact that the stories were drawn from the everyday experience of the hearers: a woman losing a coin, a man sowing seed, workers in a vineyard, shepherds tending their sheep and so on. Because the stories are set so firmly in their social context, they inevitably lose their freshness for modern hearers whose social context is different. Hence there are the occasional and largely unsuccessful attempts to retell the stories placing them in factories and supermarkets. Bible background is an attempt to make things come alive for children. Some people see Bible background as an 'escape' from religious education into a minor aspect of ancient history. It certainly can be if it is done for its own sake. However, if a teacher feels that children ought to have some special knowledge and understanding of the life and teaching of Jesus, then some study of his world is an almost essential adjunct for two reasons:

(a) so that Jesus can be seen as a real person in a real world with real feelings living in real houses with real problems ... rather than the rather 'holy' and static picture conveyed, perhaps, by scenes from stained glass windows;

(b) that for children to gain some insight into the teaching of Jesus they need some knowledge of his social world.

Areas of Bible background which teachers might choose are:

occupations
homes
furniture
clothing and jewellery
food

toys
schooling
the synagogues
the landscape
Jerusalem

Some of these areas would be more appropriate to different ages. Toys and games for example would be more suitable with very young children and a much more complex and thematic treatment of 'Jerusalem' with much older children.

An approach which many have found successful to take as a theme: '*A child's day*'. This would cut across the areas listed above and would give children an opportunity to make comparison with their own experience. A teacher of 8-year-olds worked through the following items:

1 Getting up in the morning — where did they sleep? did they have beds?
2 Getting washed and dressed — what did they wear? What did they wash with?
3 Helping with the chores — getting the water from the well, tending the animals, sweeping up.
4 Going out to play — games that were played.
5 Going to synagogue school — learning to read, teaching methods, reading the scriptures.
6 Enjoying an evening meal. What sort of food was eaten? How was it prepared? How did people eat together?

The question often arises as to how we know about life at the time of Jesus. There are three main sources and one factor which helps considerably with interpreting the other three.

Firstly, there is considerable evidence to be gleaned from the gospels themselves. A clear picture is given of aspects of farming and vine growing from the careful reading of the parables of Jesus. It is also clear that houses had flat rooves and outside staircases from the story of the paralysed man whose friends let him down through the roof (Mark, chapter 2, verses 1–12).

Secondly, archaeology of major sites in Israel has revealed a considerable wealth of information about life around the time of Jesus. The excavations at Masada and at Qumran have been considered in some detail.

An Approach Through Bible Background

Thirdly, there are the writings of historians like Josephus, the Jewish historian, and Pliny, the Roman historian. In specific cases these throw light upon the world of Jesus.

Another factor which can help considerably in interpreting evidence from these three sources is life in Israel today. In some parts of that region life has changed little and it is possible to see houses, farming methods, clothing as they were 2000 years ago. Providing this is used with caution it can be very illuminating for a study of life at the time of Jesus.

The case studies of Masada and the Dead Sea Scrolls have been developed partly as examples of how we know what life was like then and partly as ways in which Bible background can be taught in lively and interesting ways.

Bible Theme: Shepherds

The second reason for spending time in building up a picture in children's minds of life at the time of Jesus was to help them to gain some insight into his teaching. When God is talked about in the Bible, metaphors are used, arising out of human experience to describe him. Hence he is called father, judge, king, lord and so on. One very persistent metaphor of God in the Old Testament, and used by Jesus himself, is that of shepherd: 'I am the good shepherd'. Jesus was not in a literal way a shepherd. What the metaphor is intending to convey is that his relationship with people is like that of a shepherd with his sheep.

This is a powerful image for people who have experience of shepherds but for most people in the industrial west who have no direct experience of shepherds and perhaps only of sheep from the window of a motor car, the metaphor is not striking. A possible approach is to explore the notions of sheep and shepherds so as to enrich the children's experience and so to provide a basis for understanding.

The Shepherd and his Sheep (for 7–8-year-olds)

Aims

(i) To help the children to gain understanding and insight into the life and work of a shepherd in New Testament times;

(ii) to provide the tools for the children to see more perceptively into the significance of shepherd as a religious symbol.

Sheep and Shepherds Today

(i) Where are sheep found: farm fields, downland, moors.
(ii) What sort of conditions do they require for healthy living?
(iii) Possible predators: dogs, foxes, larger birds of prey.
(iv) Products from sheep: meat, lamb and mutton, wool, sheepskins: for rugs or clothing, lanolin creams.
(v) The work of the shepherd: protecting, guarding, the shepherd's crook, special consideration of a shepherd's work at lambing time.
(vi) The work of sheep dogs.

Sheep and Shepherds at the Time of Jesus

An approach here might be to select relevant passages from the Bible to build up a picture of the shepherd's job.

John, chapter 10, verses 1–6, 11–14, is a good basis for starting:

— sheepfold — a protected area surrounded by walls with a guarded entrance.

The relationship of the shepherd with his sheep:

— they know his voice and they respond to it
— the shepherd knows each of the sheep by name
— the shepherd leads his sheep (as opposed to driving) and they follow him
— the commitment of the shepherd to his sheep even to the extent of giving his life.

Luke, chapter 15, verses 3–7 'The Lost Sheep':

— this reinforces the notion of the shepherd's concern for his sheep and his preparedness to take risks to save it.

Luke, chapter 2, verse 8:

— this story of the shepherds coming to the stable at Bethlehem presents a picture of shepherds sleeping out in the fields guarding their sheep.

An Approach Through Bible Background

Psalm 23, verse 1:

This presents a picture of the shepherd leading his sheep to fresh grass, to water and to safe places.

Samuel 1, chapter 17, verses 34-36, 40:

Here the future King David as a youth leaves his father's sheep to come to King Saul's aid in his wars against the Philistines. It reveals something of the work of a shepherd

— the role in protecting the flock from predators like lions and bears;
— the use of the sling as a weapon.

It might be useful to draw in additional material too from modern times. The story of Mohammed the Wolf who accidently rediscovered the Dead Sea Scrolls (although he was a *goatherd* there are close parallels) would be illuminating.

13 Understanding the Bible

Teachers' Notes

When the question is asked by children (and adults too) of a story 'Is it true?' what they usually tend to mean is 'Did it really happen?'. This can, of course, cause considerable problems when it comes to the Bible, and equally to other sacred books as well. The 8-year-old browsing in an encyclopaedia who asked his teacher which was true: the Bible's account of creation or Darwin's, illustrates this point very forcibly. The only criterion on which he was able to judge the truth or falsity of the creation stories in Genesis, chapters 1 and 2 was whether they were *historically* true or not. Was the universe created in seven days and was woman taken from man's rib? If the answer was yes then the story was true, if not, then the story was untrue. Now the large majority of Christians would not see these early chapters of the Book of Genesis as in any way a scientific account, yet *at the same time* they would want to say that they are true but in another sense: that what they said about the world and about people is profoundly true.

This highlights the fact that the Bible is made up of different types of literature which have different purposes — myths, legends, stories, prophecy, history, law, poetry, letters. It is important that children as they reach 10 years old or so should be introduced to this so as to help them to escape the trap of literalism (as instanced above) into which they will almost certainly wander. This will enable them to move into a more mature understanding of biblical literature. The aim is not that they will accept the truth of the Bible but that they can appreciate it in a much fuller and more complex way and not reject it for inadequate reasons.

Myths

In this context myth is not used in the everyday way of describing an untrue story but in the sense of a story which intends to convey a truth. There are many stories of this ilk — why the robin has a red breast, how the leopard got its spots, why the giraffe has a long neck and so on. These all are stories to explain some phenomenon in the world around. More developed myths can be found among the Greeks. The story of Persephone gives an account of why there are seasons, seed time and harvest.

A particularly interesting Greek myth is that of Pandora and the whispering box. This can be found in most collections of Greek myths. Briefly told, the story is about a young woman, Pandora, who lives in the newly-made world, a world of joy and happiness, without pain, sorrow or disease. In this paradise she lives a carefree life of bliss with her husband and their friends. This is interrupted by the arrival of the messenger of the gods, Hermes, carrying a heavy box. He asks Pandora and her husband if he might leave it with them for a few days until he can collect it. The only condition is that it must not be opened! Pandora is obsessed by the thought of the contents of the box. She sits by it, she pours over it, she speculates about its contents and she becomes convinced that whatever is inside is alive and is begging her to let it out. She is reminded of the god's prohibition but in the end can resist no longer. She opens the box. Instantly out pour unpleasant fly-like creatures which sting Pandora and her companions. Their laughter turns to shouts of pain and they turn on each other in anger. In panic Pandora slams the box shut but it is too late — the bearers of pain, disease and unhappiness are already released into the world. Only one creature remains in the box and this Pandora also sets free. This is gentle and mothlike and flies from one to another healing their stings. This last creature is Hope!

At a superficial level this is a pleasant story but a closer look suggests that it is offering an analysis of why there is pain, discord and disharmony in the world. Why is it that there is warfare and conflict? This analysis places the cause firmly *within* people: in their disobedience to the divine command, in their pride and self-centredness. This myth of Pandora is the means of communicating this analysis.

The Creation stories in Genesis, chapters 1, 2 and 3 operate in the same sort of way. Chapter 1 with its magnificent account of creation in six days is concerned with three main issues: that there is *purpose* in creation ('and God said "let there be light" etc.') — it did not just happen; that there is *order* in creation, that the creation, the physical world, is *good* ('and God saw that it was good!). Chapter 2, which is in fact a second account of creation, differing in some respects of order from the first account, emphasizes the creation of man and his relationship to the created order and to woman. It introduces too the picture of the Garden of Eden, an earthly paradise of harmony and peace. This paves the way for the story of the Fall in chapter 3. The writer wants to account for the difference between the human situation we all experience which compasses suffering, disease, death and disharmony and that which must have been in the intention of a loving creator (as symbolized by Eden). He frames this analysis in the story of the eating of the forbidden fruit from the tree of the knowledge of good and evil. The serpent tempts the woman to eat the fruit with the words 'you shall not surely die: for God doth know that in the day you ate thereof, then your eyes shall be opened, and you shall be as gods, knowing good and evil' (Genesis, chapter 3, verse 5). In other words, the analysis places the cause firmly within people: the cause is human pride, its desire to be always at the centre. This, the story suggests, is at the root of human problems.

When we want to ask questions about the truth of these stories we are not therefore asking whether there was a Garden of Eden, a first man and woman or a tree of the knowledge of good and evil but whether the analysis of why things are as they are is true or helpful.

Legend

A legend is usually defined as a story which has a basis in history but which has become exaggerated. Examples of this are the stories of such figures as Robin Hood and Davy Crockett ('killed him a bear when he was only three').

Given the ancient literature in parts of the Bible and allowing for a period of oral transmission, it would be surprising if the Bible did not contain examples. Samson is perhaps the outstanding example. An Israelite folk hero, Samson was renowned for his courage and for his considerable strength. He is best known for his battles against the Philistines, his relationship with Delilah and the connection between his strength and his uncut hair. Among the stories which are recorded about him in the Book of Judges, chapters 13–16 are two which seem to have the touch of legend about them.

Judges, chapter 15, verses 14–17

Samson is bound by his fellow countrymen and handed over to the Philistines who are ruling over the country. When he is delivered to the Philistines he breaks his bonds and seeing a new jaw bone of an ass lying on the ground, he picks it up to use as a weapon. And with the weapon he slew *one thousand* men.

Judges, chapter 16, verses 1–3

Samson's overnight presence in Gaza is noticed by the inhabitants who plot to kill him at dawn. Samson rises from bed at midnight and finding the city gates locked, picks up the doors of the gates of the city with the two posts and with the bar as well and, hoisting them on to his shoulders, carries them to the top of the hill by Hebron.

There is nothing surprising that there should be legends: it is just something to bear in mind.

Stories

There are in the Bible a number of books which were written for a special purpose and were not intended to be historical accounts. Notable among these are the books of Jonah, Ruth and Daniel. All are firmly embedded in the historical situations in which they were written and, as this is largely unfamiliar to most modern readers, it is not surprising that their purpose is misunderstood.

Jonah and Ruth both appear to arise out of the same series of events in the history of Israel. Briefly told, in 587 BC the Kingdom of Judah was overcome by Nebuchadnezzar, Jerusalem was captured and the people taken into exile in Babylon, hundreds of miles from their native land. It was a time of great bitterness for the Jewish people and also a time of much religious questioning. Why had God allowed this to happen to His chosen people? Was He less powerful than the gods of Babylon? With the help of their prophets the Jewish people came to see purpose in their exile. It was not a sign of God's weakness, rather of his power and uniqueness. Rather it was a punishment on them for their complacency and their unwillingness to share their knowledge of God among the nations. The prophet who above all fostered this is unknown to us by name and is referred to as Second Isaiah or Isaiah of Babylon, as his writings appear in the prophecy of Isaiah, chapters 40 to 55. He speaks towards the end of the sixty years of exile. The Jewish people, he says, have learnt their lesson and God has forgiven them (Isaiah, chapter 40, verse 1). He speaks of God working through the events of history. Just as he caused the Jews to go into exile so he is now arranging the events for their return. He is raising up a young king, Cyrus, who will overthrow the Babylonian empire and replace it with his own, the Persian empire. He will permit the Jews to return to their land to rebuild Jerusalem and fulfil their vocation as the chosen people to bring the knowledge of God to the whole world.

In 537 Cyrus allowed the Jews to return. Not all did, as many had put down deep roots in Babylon and after sixty years of exile few were alive who had clear memories of home. Those that did return went with high hopes to live out their vocation. However, the high hopes faded. Jerusalem was a ruin; they were not welcomed by either those who lived among the ruins nor those who ruled the province from their seat in Samaria; there was a succession of poor harvests. Life became a battle for survival and for safety's sake this meant that top priority must be given to the rebuilding of the walls of Jerusalem. The rebuilding of the walls became symbolic of what was happening to the restored community. It turned increasingly inward and the vision of the spreading of the knowledge of God among the nations faded. Maintaining the *purity* of the faith became pre-eminent; the law was rigorously enforced and there were purges of people who did not meet the necessary criteria. This religious exclusiveness culminated in the requirement that all Jewish males who had married foreign wives must divorce them and these women must leave the community. So the wheel had come full circle. The only difference between the Jews at this point and those before the exile was that the current ones were even more exclusive.

These developments did not meet with the approval of all and there were some who stood in the universalist tradition of Second Isaiah. The *Book of Ruth* serves in particular as a strong protest against the compulsory divorcing of foreign wives. It is the story of a Moabite woman (therefore a foreigner) of singular grace, beauty, gentleness, faith and compassion who was also the great grandmother of the great King David. She would have been put away too!

The *Book of Jonah* is a more complex allegory. It is the story of a Jew whom God told to go and preach at Nineveh (a symbol of pagan power). Rather than do this he fled to Joppa and took ship for Tarshish. But a great storm arose which threatened to sink the ship so the sailors cast lots to see who was the cause of this. The lot fell on Jonah who confessed that he was fleeing from God's will and asked them to throw him into the sea. They did so and the storm ceased. Meanwhile the Lord had prepared a big fish to swallow up Jonah. This it duly did and Jonah spent three days in its belly during which time he repented of his actions. The big fish then vomited up Jonah on the shore and he proceeded straight to Nineveh where he preached so successfully that they repented in sackcloth and ashes — so much so that the Lord forgave their extreme wickedness. This angered Jonah who went away and sulked. The Lord chides him for his lack of pity.

This in allegorical form is the history and direction of the Jewish people. The refusal to spread the knowledge of God (Jonah's flight), the terrible conquest by the Babylonians (the fearful storm at sea), the exile and the change of heart (the three days and nights inside the fish) the return to Jerusalem (Jonah vomited up by the fish). Then comes the parting of the ways. Jonah does preach but is angry and sulks and God chides him. Here is the message to the readers of the day. The plea to keep fast to their universalistic principles. Seen in this context, discussions about whether a person can survive for seventy-two hours inside a fish misses the point!

The *Book of Daniel*, which contains the well-known stories of Daniel in the lions' den and of Shadrach, Meshach and Abed-nego in the burning fiery furnace, arises in a very different historical setting. It was written during the reign of the Seleucid emperor, Antiochus Epiphanes (175–163 BC) by an unknown writer who wrote to his contemporaries through the mouth of one, Daniel, who is set in the court of Babylon during the Jewish exile.

The immediate crisis was one of intense persecution. Antiochus ruled a large empire of which Israel was only a small part. In an attempt to create a greater sense of unity throughout his diverse empire, Antiochus actively encouraged the spread of Hellenism (the Greek way of life). Most of his subjugated people took to this quite readily. They renamed their gods by Greek names, they began to use the newly-built gymnasia. A number of Jews cheerfully adopted such a way but pious Jews were horrified and would not cooperate. Antiochus reacted by forbidding the practice of the Jewish religion and by taking the Temple in Jerusalem in 167 BC where he erected a pagan altar in the Holy of Holies and sacrificed pigs' flesh which to Jews was unclean meat. This desecration was seen by faithful Jews as the 'abomination of desolation'. Jews who refused to comply were treated very savagely. The first book of the Maccabees in the Apocrypha (those books between the Old and New Testaments) describes the period in great detail. The faithful Jews did not remain passive. Under Judas Maccabeus many revolted and resisted Antiochus Epiphanes with great courage (mainly through guerilla warfare).

It was to this situation of faithful Jews, in a tiny minority against a large and powerful Empire bent upon their destruction that the Book of Daniel is addressed. Just through their courage, fortitude and skill they won through and in December 164 BC the temple was cleansed and restored to the worship of God. (It is this event which the Jewish festival of Chanukkah celebrates.) The message is clear: that God will not let the persecution last for long. Israel is the chosen People of God and He will not allow them to be destroyed. The secret is to remain faithful and God will protect and save. Hence in the story of Shadrach, Meshach and Abed-nego, (Daniel, chapter 3), King Nebuchadnezzar erects a golden statue to which all are commanded to bow down and to worship whenever they hear the sound of certain musical instruments. The three Jews, who are all officials of the king, refuse to do so because the Jewish religion forbids it. In his anger, the king orders that the penalty for disobedience to the command be implemented and the three Jews are thrown into the burning fiery furnace which has been heated to seven times its usual heat. Yet in the furnace, God was with them and nothing of them was burned. The king issues a proclamation that no one must speak amiss of the God of Shadrach, Meshach and Abed-nego. So faithfulness to God and to his commands is vindicated.

In a similar way, Daniel himself disobeys the command (Daniel, chapter 6) that no-one for thirty days should ask a petition of any God or man except for the king on pain of being thrown into a den of lions. Daniel continues his normal practice of praying in his window and his enemies report him to the king, to the king's great distress. The king has no choice because the law of the Medes and the Persians cannot be altered. So Daniel is cast into the lions' den. During the night the lions do not touch Daniel and he comes out unharmed. And so the God of Daniel is honoured. Again it is the same message of faithfulness and vindication. Daniel was faithful to God and God protected him. These were powerful messages to the Jews who were resisting Antiochus.

Prophecy

A particular mark of the Old Testament is prophecy. Contrary to the current notion that a prophet is one who can see into the future and tell what is to be, the Old Testament prophet was much more a spokesman to his own people and generation about the present time. To over-simplify, the Old Testament prophet was a forthteller rather than a foreteller!

Now it is certainly true that there were prophets in Israel who could be consulted as fortune tellers but this style of prophecy was rejected by the great prophets. When the prophet Amos is called a prophet by Amaziah, the priest of Bethel, he reacts speedily 'I was no prophet neither was a prophet's son' (Amos, chapter 7, verse 14). The prophet believed that he was supremely the instrument of God in speaking to his own generation. When speaking an oracle to the people the prophet usually prefaced it with the words 'Thus saith the Lord' emphasizing therefore his or her role as a mouthpiece of God.

Amos is perhaps the most straightforward of the prophets to understand. From Tekoa he was by occupation a herdsman and a tender of sycamore trees. He believed that God had called him out to go and speak His word to Israel. The situation was that the people of Israel had largely forgotten their distinctive way of life as the chosen people. There was a great disparity of wealth between the rich and the poor and although all were brother Israelites, there was very little concern about it. Moreover there was bribery in the courts so that the poor had little opportunity of getting justice there. There was slavery in the land — it was possible to buy a slave for the price of a pair of shoes. Amos paints pictures of the wealthy citizens laying on their ivory beds, eating the best lambs and calves, anointing themselves with the best ointments and drinking bowls of wine. The harshest words came for the women of the capital city, Samaria, 'Hear this word, ye kine of Bashan[1], that are in the mountains of Samaria, which oppress the poor, which crush the needy, which say to their masters "Bring, and let us drink"' (Amos, chapter 4, verse 1). 'The word of the Lord' which Amos brings is one of judgment but with the appeal 'Seek me and ye shall live' (Amos, chapter 5, verse 4). Unless this happens there will be the 'Day of the Lord' a day of judgment which will be mediated through outside military forces. The country will be overun and the people taken captive. This is a note of hope in Amos. In his final chapter (if it is not a later addition) he points to a time when an Israelite, chastened and purified by her punishment, might rebuild her life on the right lines.

Prophets were speakers rather than writers and it seems that their followers wrote down their oracles, the memory aided by the tradition of prophets speaking in poetic form. Often their oracles are not written down in a logical sequence and this can be confusing to readers. Prophets inevitably were unpopular figures in their own day and it is possible that one, Jeremiah, might have been murdered. But such is the fate of prophets in all ages including our own!

Old Testament prophets include Hosea, Isaiah of Jerusalem (Isaiah, chapters 1–39 inclusive), Isaiah of Babylon (Isaiah, chapters 40–55) Ezekiel, Jeremiah and Micah. The message of each one is inevitably tied very closely to the historical and social situation of the day.

History

Although the point has been made earlier that the Bible is not all history, this does not mean that some of it is not history. In fact, the biblical drama is set in the context of history, beginning with the Patriarchs, Abraham, Isaac and Jacob, through Moses, the monarchy and right through to the life of Jesus and the activity of St. Paul. This historical story is acted out against the background of the history of the great world empires, the Sumerian, Assyrian, Babylonian, Persian, Greek and Roman, always there and often appearing directly on the stage.

Generally speaking the history in the Bible is corroborated by other contemporary accounts unearthed by archaeologists. For example, in the reign of Hezekiah, King of Judah (715–687/6 BC) the Assyrian Emperor, Sennacherib, came up against Judah so overwhelmingly that Hezekiah sued for peace, offering a much larger annual tribute (2 Kings, chapter 18, verses 13 onwards). This was accepted by Sennacherib. Reference is found to this in the Assyrian annals:

> As for Hezekiah the Jew, who did not submit to my yoke, forty-six of his strong walled cities in their neighbourhood ... I besieged and took ... Himself, like a caged bird, I shut up in Jerusalem, his royal city ... As for Hezekiah, the terrifying splendour of my majesty overcame him ... and his mercenary troops ... deserted him.[2]

This was but a breathing space while Hezekiah set about strengthening the defensive position of Jerusalem. 2 Kings, chapter 20, verse 20 talks about the acts of Hezekiah and about 'how he made a pool and a conduit and brought water into the city'. This conduit was uncovered in 1880 and from this discovery it is possible to describe the tunnel very clearly.

This is quoted in some detail to show that historical writing in the Bible tends to find corroboration from other sources. This, of course, does not prove the truth of the faith of the Bible but it does show that where it is intending to write history the biblical texts are reasonably accurate.

There is one further point to make about the history in the Bible. It is *interpreted* history or *theological* history. The biblical faith is that God is constantly active in the world. History is the arena of his operation. Hence when something happens it is because God causes it to happen. Hence, to refer back to the material earlier on the exile in the chapter under 'Stories', the modern historian might note that the

Jewish people were taken into exile in Babylon by Nebuchadnezzar and account for it in terms of the strength of Babylon, the comparative weakness of Egypt and so on. The biblical writers were much more concerned to account for why God had caused it to happen, in other words to interpret it to discover his purposes.

Law

Within the Old Testament there is a considerable concern for law, that is for the requirements which God requires of humans. At the heart of the Old Testament faith is the notion of Covenant. This means an agreement freely entered into by God and Israel with requirements on both sides. The divine undertaking is contained in the words 'I will be their God'. The human side involves an undertaking to obey the divine commands. These are expressed centrally in the Ten Commandments (Exodus, chapter 20) and form the core of the *moral* law. There is also the *ritual* law which laid down regulations about the worship of the community.

Poetry

The best known poems in the Bible are the Psalms, 150 in number, which figure prominently in worship. They come from many sources: some are songs of praise, others of deriliction; some arise out of specific historical situations. *Psalm 148*, for example, is a song of praise. *Psalm 24* is thought by many scholars to rise out of a particular situation. The second part of the Psalm reads (verses 7–8)

> Lift up your heads, O ye gates;
> And be ye lift up ye everlasting doors;
> And the king of glory shall come in.
> Who is this king of glory?
> The Lord strong and mighty,
> The Lord mighty in battle

It has been suggested that this Psalm relates to the entry of the Ark into Jerusalem. The 'question and answer' style suggests too an antiphonal versical and response between the priests and the people.

Psalm 137 clearly arises from the period of the Exile in Babylon. It expresses the deep sadness of exile, the deep devotion to Jerusalem and the deep bitterness towards their captors.

Another book of poetry, known as the Song of Solomon or the Song of Songs, is a collection of love poetry. It has often been interpreted, perhaps rather piously, as an allegory of the love between Christ and the church, but it does have a rather more carnal flavour about it!

Letters

Much of the New Testament consists of letters (or epistles) written by leaders in the church. Notable among these are St Paul, St Peter and St John. The letters were normally written to one or other of the small churches scattered around the Mediterranean and deal with problems which had arisen and were causing disagreements. Should Christians eat meat which had been first sacrificed to idols? How should Christians behave in a hostile environment? Sometimes they were written to admonish. The Corinthian church was remarkably quarrelsome and this worried Paul and so he wrote to chide its members. Our only way of knowing this though is by a careful reading of the letters as this is our only source of information.

The shortest epistle in the New Testament is that of Paul to Philemon about one, Onesimus, a runaway slave.

Approaches in the Classroom

Myths

Aims

To help the children:

(i) to have some understanding of the meaning of myth;
(ii) to perceive that most Christians agree that in the Bible mythological material is one of the means of conveying truth;
(iii) to explore the sort of truth conveyed by myth;
(iv) to investigate a few specific examples.

Possible Approach

1 Read a number of myths to the children drawn if possible from a variety of sources, for example, Loki and the Mistletoe

(Norse), Phaeton and the Sun Chariot (Greek), Pandora and the Whispering Box (Greek).
2. Select the story of Pandora and discuss in detail what it is about. Distinguish between historical literal truth and mythological truth.
3. Discuss the sorts of myths which might be useful today and get the children to write their own.
4. Introduce the notions of myth in the Bible.
Read with the children the two creation stories, Genesis, chapter 1, verse 1 to chapter 2, verse 4a; Genesis, chapter 2, verse 4b to end. Discuss with the children in detail what they are seeking to convey.
5. Study the story of the Garden of Eden (Genesis, chapter 3). Discuss what it is saying about the relationship of humans to the created order, about the roots of conflict, suffering and strife.

Legends

Aims

To help the children:
(i) to have some understanding of the meaning of legend;
(ii) to realize how widespread is legend;
(iii) to identify legendary elements in biblical literature;
(iv) to investigate a few specific examples.

Possible Approach

1. Read a number of legends about well known figures, for example, Robin Hood, Davy Crockett. Discuss ways in which legends arise.
2. Select a figure like James Bond, a contemporary though fictional figure. Discuss with the children which of his exploits could be factual and which would be legendary.
3. Identify contemporary figures (in political life, entertainment, sport etc.) and consider how legendary stories might develop about them.
4. Get the children to write their own legends about historical or contemporary figures.

Religious Education 5–12

5 Consider legendary elements in biblical literature with a special focus upon the Samson stories.

Stories (with special reference to the Book of Daniel)

Aims

To help the children:
- (i) to see more deeply into the Book of Daniel;
- (ii) to relate the meaning of the book to its historical setting;
- (iii) to enter sympathetically into the historical setting;
- (iv) to explore the ideas of faith and resistance.

Possible Approach

1. Describe an enemy occupied country. What would it be like to live in such a setting? Discuss the role of resistance movements working underground (for example, France, Norway): patriotism, isolation, dangers, sabotage, difficulties of communication, development of secret codes and spies. Encourage the children to invent codes etc.
2. Begin to describe the similar situation in Palestine about 170 BC:
    - (a) occupied by the Seleucid emperor, Antiochus Epiphanes;
    - (b) his policy of Hellenizing his empire;
    - (c) the resistance of devout Jews in Palestine;
    - (d) Antiochus' proscripton of the Jewish religion and his treatment of the Temple;
    - (e) the revolt of Judas Maccabeus;
    - (f) Victory over Antiochus and the reconsecration of the Temple.
3. Read extracts from books of the period, notably the first and second books of the Maccabees (to be found in the Apocrypha). 2 Maccabees, chapter 6, verses 18–31 recounts the ill treatment of a respected Jewish elder who refused to eat pork, a meat forbidden under Jewish law. 2 Maccabees, chapter 7 recounts a similiar tale but even more horrendously. 2 Maccabees, chapter 1, verses 60–61 and chapter 6, verse 10 record other incidents of persecution.
4. Through discussion, writing or drama, help the children to enter into this situation imaginatively. What must it have been

Understanding the Bible

like to live in such a time? What would give people such resolve to remain faithful?

5 Introduce the Book of Daniel
Read Daniel chapter 6 (the Lions' Den) with the children. How might it have been of help at such a time.

Repeat the process with Daniel chapter 3 (the Burning Fiery Furness) and with Daniel chapter 5 (Belshazzar's Feast). What themes do they have? How might they be of value?

Prophecy

Aims

To help the children;

(i) to gain some understanding of the role of the prophet in ancient Israel;
(ii) to gain some knowledge of one prophet;
(iii) to begin to identify prophets in the contemporary world.

Possible Approach

1 Prophets as forthtellers and not foretellers. Contrast with fortune tellers at fairgrounds.
2 Read an extract from one of the prophets (for example, Isaiah, chapter 5) to illustrate the use of prophetic oracles of speaking.
3 Consideration of the call of a prophet — a conviction that they were specially chosen by God (for example, Isaiah, chapter 6, verses 1–8 for perhaps the most dramatic call)
4 Refer to a number of the prophets of Israel, finding their books in the Old Testament.
5 Take a case study — Amos. Encourage the children to search through the Book of Amos in order that they can build up a picture of the society to which Amos spoke. What did he condemn? Why did he condemn it?
6 A consideration of the things that prophets might say to modern society.
7 A study of an acclaimed contemporary prophet, for example, Mother Teresa, Trevor Huddleston, Helder Camara.

Notes

1 Kine (cows) of Bashan were the plumpest and sleekest in the country.
2 This material is drawn from R.K. HARRISON 'Archaeology of the Old Testament' Hodder and Stoughton (1963). This has much material of this kind and is a very valuable source of information.

14 Teaching About Jesus

Any discussion with a group of teachers about work with young children on the life of Jesus shows that it is a controversial area. There is the clear problem for many teachers that the historical events of the life of Jesus are inseparable from a religious interpretation of them: that Jesus is the Son of God is assumed in the New Testament accounts. Some of the concepts too are difficult: teachers of very young children often have great difficulty in explaining what angels are to the more persistent of their young questioners. There are uncertainties about the helpfulness of telling miracle stories and parables. Very frequently these problems are resolved by a process of ignoring — either the life of Jesus or the perceived problems!

What Do We Know About Jesus?

What we know of the historical Jesus comes to us from the pages of the New Testament and principally from the four gospels of Matthew, Mark, Luke and John. As far as we know there are no contemporary references to Jesus in Greek, Roman or Jewish sources though there are later (brief) references in Suetonius, Tacitus, Pliny and Josephus.

In the New Testament, apart from the four gospels, there is very little interest shown in the life of Jesus, excluding his death and resurrection. St Paul, for example, is much more concerned with the significance of Jesus in the saving purpose of God than with what he said or did in Palestine. It is in the gospels that we get the only detail.

Although there are only four gospels in the New Testament, many others were written, often long after the events, which did not find their way into the New Testament. They form part of a great deposit of pious writing, including also lives of the Virgin Mary, which grew up in various parts of the Christian church. For school purposes it seems best to restrict our attention to the four authoritative gospels.

If we are looking for an account of the life of Jesus, then we are bound to be disappointed. Gospels are not biographies. Gospel means literally 'good news' and so, for example, St Mark's gospel is really 'The Good News of Jesus Christ according to St Mark'. Gospels therefore are proclamations. John, towards the end of his gospel, makes this very clear.

> These (ie stories) are written that you might believe that Jesus is the Son of God; and that believing you might have life through his name (John, chapter 20, verse 31).

Gospels are therefore works with a confessional purpose and the material they include is selected for that end. Mark, for example, the earliest gospel to be written, begins with Jesus at the age of 30, at the start of his mission. Matthew and Luke start the story much earlier with the birth of Jesus because they clearly feel this to be significant in their presentation of Jesus. Matthew, for instance, seems to be writing for a Jewish audience and so one of his purposes is to present Jesus as the expected one who fulfils the hopes of the Jewish people. His account of Jesus' birth is full of quotations from the Old Testament to show that Jesus is the one who fulfils the old prophecies. Luke dedicates his gospel to one, Theophilus, clearly a non-Jew, and the tone of his gospel is very different with material selected appropriate to his purpose. It is only in Luke that we get the parables of the Good Samaritan and the Prodigal Son and the story of Zacchaeus, selected presumably by Luke to reflect Jesus' concern for those outside the normative Judaism of his day — a theme which would be of particular relevance to Greek and Roman readers.

The gospel writers therefore selected their material very carefully for a purpose and that purpose was to convince their readers that the person of whom they were reading was none other than the Son of God. The events, carefully selected, are therefore permeated by this conviction. It is very difficult to separate the Jesus of history from the Christ of faith.

It is clear too that underlying the events recorded in the gospels are difficult and complicated themes. Jesus is not another prophet; anyone who sees Jesus has seen God. Jesus' death on the cross is not just another sad end to a noble man (like Socrates); it is the most significant event in the history of the world. Jesus is not just to be followed as a moral teacher who presented a compassionate and loving way of life, anyone who possesses him possesses eternal life.

Teaching About Jesus

These considerations tend to make the gospels into books for adults rather than for children. This, of course, does not mean that all the stories of the life of Jesus are unsuitable for children. It does however place the onus upon teachers, when they select stories to tell to their children, to ask themselves whether the stories in question will be *stepping stones* or *stumbling blocks* to a *mature* understanding of the life and significance of Jesus.

What About Miracles?

The gospels are full of stories of miracles, be they stories of healing, raisings from the dead or nature miracles, using miracle in the sense of an event for which there is no readily available natural explanation. That there are many miracles recorded in the gospels is not surprising because, to people of the time of Jesus, the working of miracles was a sign of special power or authority. It was not that miracles were unique to Jesus; miraculous workings are recorded of many other figures in the ancient world.

An unusual feature in the teaching of Jesus, however, is a definite attempt to cast a veil of secrecy over the miracles. Jesus did not want to attract followers merely because they were impressed by his miracles. His motive was not to impress but always invariably lay in his compassion: seeing a widowed mother burying her only son and so on. The miracles nevertheless are presented in the gospels as signs, at least for those with eyes to see! 'If I with the finger of God cast out devils, then the Kingdom of God is come upon you' (Luke, chapter 11, verse 20). The miracles were seen as evidence that Jesus, in his ministry, was driving back the powers of evil.

The miracle stories pose a number of problems to modern readers. There is the problem that many of the thought forms of the world in which Jesus lived and in which the gospels were written are different from those most have today. This is particularly significant in two ways: in the notion of devil possession and in the general attitude towards the miraculous. A number of the healing miracle stories are tied up with the concept of devil possession. There was a pervasive view in the ancient world that there were personal evil powers (devils) who were in a constant state of warfare with God: evil versus good. When they could, these devils or demons entered into individuals and possessed them. The story of the Gadarene demoniac (Luke, chapter 8, verses 26–40) is a good example of this. Most people today would be more inclined to interpret these stories as instances of various mental or physical illnesses rather than subscribe to the notion of demon possession. Older children can look at some of these miracle stories and discuss them. Younger children are not really able to do this.

Allied with this is the general attitude to the miraculous. Whereas to the first readers of the gospels, the miracle stories would have provided a strong incentive to believe the claims about Jesus, to many readers today the miracle stories operate in the reverse way: they cast doubts in many minds about the truth of *all* the gospel stories.

This can often be detected in the thinking of young children who have had a heavy exposure to the miracle stories of Jesus. The following extract of a conversation of 6/7-year-olds was overheard in their classroom as they were making up their own play of the story of Jesus feeding the 5000 people which they had heard in assembly that morning:

Jamie: 'Who's doing the magic?'
Emma: 'I will! I will!'
Danny: 'No you can't, you can't. You're a girl. I will, I will, I will. I'm doing the magic. I'm Jesus.'

Jesus the magic man! This characterization of Jesus as a super-magician is very common among young children — and older ones too!

While it may be useful and interesting to discuss the whole idea of the miraculous with much older children, drawing on both the miracle stories in the gospels and more modern (claimed) instances at, say, Lourdes, younger children are not really able to deal with it adequately and they file it away into the compartment of their minds labelled 'magic' where it tends to stay. When teachers of younger children consider telling a series of miracle stories to their classes — and the temptation can be very great — the question again which they should ask is whether the experience will be a *stepping stone* or a *stumbling block* to a *mature* understanding of the life and significance of Jesus.

What About Parables?

Just as teachers may often decide to tell a series of stories on the miracles of Jesus so they often do the same with the parables of Jesus. After all, they are good lively stories well loved and popular and, of course, it is easy to choose one to tell each week in story time!

Because parables are stories about everyday life — or at least everyday life in the time of Jesus — and talk of vineyards, farmers sowing their seed, people travelling on donkeys and so on, it is often forgotten how difficult they are. On one hand they tell a story of everyday life but they really point to a meaning beyond that; and the problem is to move from the first level to the second. This is not a new problem: many in the crowds who heard Jesus tell the parables took them as fascinating stories. Not all, as Jesus himself put it, had eyes to see or ears to hear!

Immediately after the results of Goldman's research was made available, many teachers claimed that all parables were beyond the reasonable comprehension of children under the age of 11 or so when their thinking was beginning to cope with abstract ideas. This is certainly an overstatement but it does nevertheless make a serious point: if the parables are told so that the children can begin to understand something of the teaching of Jesus then there is a problem because they are being asked to deal with the complex exercise of taking one story and then seeing its meaning in another completely different realm.

An *example* of this might be the parable of the ten maidens (Matthew, chapter 25, verses 1–13). The story is about ten girls who took their lamps to go out to meet the bridegroom at a wedding. As the bridegroom was late in coming they all fell asleep. At midnight they were awoken by the shout that he was about to arrive and would they go out to meet him. At this point five of the girls realize that the oil in their lamps is used up and they ask the other five to lend them some. The other five whose lamps are full of oil decline to do so in case there is not enough to provide for all ten and send the foolish ones off to buy some more oil. While they are away at the shop, the bridegroom arrives and the five wise girls accompany him with their lamps into the marriage and the door is shut. When the foolish girls return with their fresh oil they find themselves excluded from the marriage.

In many ways this is a very attractive story for younger children. It involves looking at wedding customs at the time of Jesus; it has excitement of the girls falling asleep and some being caught out; it has the satisfaction in the black and white justice of the unprepared girls being excluded from the marriage. 'It serves them right' is a common response from children! However the parable is really dealing with other matters.

The parable centres around the notion of 'being ready' and is addressed to the hearers as a personal question. Underlying it is the idea of the Kingdom (or rule) of God which Jesus came to announce. At the centre of Jesus' teaching is the notion that God will break into human history and establish his reign. When that will be is unknown so people should be in a state of readiness, both moral and spiritual. Those who are not, the parable seems to be saying, will be excluded. What seems at first sight to be an interesting story of ten girls at a wedding is really an awesome warning.

Few would dispute that this story as a parable is considerably beyond the level of understanding of young children. This one is not an isolated example and most of the parables are of similar difficulty to this, so great care is necessary in the *selection* of which ones might be used.

Some of the parables are suitable for use with younger children. The Lost Coin (Luke, chapter 15, verses 8–10) and the Lost Sheep (Luke, chapter 15, verses 4–7) both have the same themes of the preciousness of the object lost, the great efforts made to find it and the great rejoicing when it was finally found and so make the same point that every individual is immensely precious to God. The parable of the Lost (or Prodigal) Son (Luke, chapter 15, verses 11–32) is similar in that it emphasizes the complete forgiveness of the father for his son who has rejected him but it also moves one step beyond to chide the pious and the good (in the figure of the elder brother) who do not share the same joy as the father! The Good Samaritan (Luke, chapter 10, verses 25–37) too with its emphasis upon caring and compassion is also suitable though it could well be looked at in more detail with the 10-year-olds and older to explore the idea of neighbourliness.

A serious problem with popular stories like the parables is one of *repetition*. The Good Samaritan and the Prodigal Son are told over and over again in class and it is quite possible to hear them fifteen to twenty times in school before the age of 12. Repetition of some stories (like the birth stories) seems, in most cases, only to increase their appeal. In other cases it can lead to boredom. Teachers need to be sensitive to this and this may mean not using a particular story with younger children if that will spoil if for a later time when it may be more appropriate. The principle again is whether the use of a particular parable is likely to be a *stepping* stone or a *stumbling* block to a mature understanding of the teaching of Jesus.

Teaching About Jesus

Possible Approaches to the Life of Jesus

Festivals

Perhaps the commonest approach to the life of Jesus is through work on the two festivals of Christmas and Easter. Practically every school does some work in preparation for Christmas and a number of approaches are suggested in detail for different age groups in the section on teaching festivals. Easter is perhaps slightly less popular in schools than Christmas but it is still very common. An approach to Easter through the use of artefacts is described in the chapter on 'resources'. There are other lesser festivals celebrating events in the life of Jesus which many schools use either in classroom work or in assembly and these are included in the chapter on 'Christian festivals'.

Background Understanding

A problem, which has been discussed at other points, in studying the life of Jesus, is the cultural difference between the world in which Jesus lived and the western world today. An important part of the teacher's task in helping younger children to develop some understanding of the life and teaching of Jesus is to introduce them to his world. Approaches to this are discussed in some detail in the section on 'Bible background' in the chapter on 'The Bible'.

The teaching of this background material would be developmental. Five-year-olds (particularly at Christmas time) might learn how babies were looked after, leading on to something of family life and the sort of house that Jesus would have inhabited in Nazareth. Twelve-year-olds on the other hand would be able to cope with a study of the various groupings who had significant parts to play in the life and ministry of Jesus such as the Pharisees, the Scribes, the Sadducees and the Zealots and to begin to question why such a hostility towards Jesus began to develop.

Who is Jesus?

Over the age range from 5–12 years there is inevitably going to be a wide range of approaches starting perhaps at 5 with the idea that Jesus was a very important man to finding at 12 a number of pupils comparing Matthew's and Luke's accounts of the birth of Jesus and discussing their respective standpoints.

With children between 5 and 7, in addition to work on the life Jesus lived (home, school, games and so on) and the normal work on festivals, Jesus should be presented under such headings as 'The Friendly Man' or 'The Man Who Cared'.

The Friendly Man

Suitable stories would include:

> Zacchaeus (Luke, chapter 19; verses 1–9) — the Roman collaborator ostracized by his fellow citizens but accepted by Jesus.
> The Little Children (Luke, chapter 18, verses 15–17) Jesus received the children his disciples had tried to send away.
> Parables such as the Lost Coin (Luke, chapter 15, verses 8–10), the Lost Sheep (Luke, chapter 15, verses 4–7) or the Prodigal Son (Luke, chapter 15, verses 11–32) — all of which emphasize the openness of God to everyone.

With older children it is useful to begin to build up the more complex picture of Jesus being loved by many for his teaching and his compassion yet at the same time becoming an object of hatred to others. Two useful stories to use in this context would be:

> The Call of Levi (Luke, chapter 5, verses 27–32)
> Jesus' feet are anointed in the house of Simon the Pharisee (Luke, chapter 7, verses 36–40).

This can be further developed with 10-year-olds and above by looking at the plots hatched by some of the religious leaders to have Jesus executed.

Friends of Jesus

Other approaches particularly with young children could be 'Friends of Jesus' — suitable stories could include:

His disciples: for example,	
Simon Peter and Andrew	Mark, chapter 1, verses 16–20
	Luke, chapter 5, verses 1–11
Levi/Matthew	Luke, chapter 5, verses 27–32
Little children:	Luke, chapter 18, verses 15–17

Teaching About Jesus

Zacchaeus: Luke, chapter 19, verses 1–9
Mary and Martha: Luke, chapter 10, verses 38–41
Joseph of Arimathaea: Luke, chapter 23, verses 50–56
The man who lent his donkey: Luke, chapter 19, verses 28–40

With older children it is possible to develop this work by looking more closely at the implications of being a 'Friend of Jesus' with particular regard to the idea of 'discipleship'.

With older children in addition to the two approaches already described which can be developed for children in the nine plus age group, other approaches to 'who is Jesus' can be developed.

Jesus the Messiah

One of the most startling features of the gospel is Jesus' reluctance to answer direct questions about the origin of his authority.

A good starting point would be the highly symbolic story of the Temptations of Jesus (Luke, chapter 4, verses 1–13) in which he is confronted with three different approaches to his ministry, all of which he rejects.

This could be linked in with the expectations of messiahship which were current at that period.

Jesus the Miracle Worker

With children able to deal with the issues, it would be sensible to consider miracles perhaps by exploring the following questions:

What do we understand by miracles?
Any contemporary examples heard by the pupils?
Distinguish between healing miracles and nature miracles?
What motives do the gospel writers attribute to Jesus in performing the miracles?
How do we respond to them?
What of the claimed miracles at shrines such as Lourdes?

Jesus the Teacher

With children aged 11–12 a valuable approach to explore an aspect of the teaching of Jesus would be to study and discuss selections from the Sermon on the Mount (Matthew, chapters 5–7)

>The Beatitudes (Matthew, chapter 5, verses 1–12)
>Salt and Light (Matthew, chapter 5, verses 13–16)
>The New Law — goodness lies in the heart not just in outward action.
>'Thou shalt not kill' (Matthew, chapter 5, verses 21–22)
>'Love your enemies' (Matthew, chapter 5, verses 43–48)
>Real Religion: against being a hypocrite, almsgiving, praying and fasting (Matthew, chapter 6, verses 1–18)
>Don't be anxious: (Matthew, chapter 6, verses 24–34)
>Parables of the rock and the sand (Matthew, chapter 7, verses 24–29)

In this approach there is always present the great danger of slipping over into sentimentality. This can be easily avoided but it is best to bear it in mind.

Parables

It has been noted already how complex some of the parables are and that even those which are within the grasp of children of 10 years of age and more are often spoiled by frequent repetition. One teacher of a class of 11-year-olds confronted with this situation, describes how she dealt with it:

>My class is not one that could be described as easy. In fact, I think that in my ten years of teaching it is the most difficult I have had. During the autumn term there was considerable concern among the school governors and the teaching staff about the instances of 'racist' behaviour in the school. The staff agreed to adopt a number of strategies some of which might be described as direct and others indirect. One of my strategies was to focus some of my teaching upon the theme of neighbourliness, to link this with RE and, as far as I could, to try to involve as much discussion work as possible. I began with the Christian principle 'love your neighbour as yourself' and tried to explore with the class the meaning of the term 'love'. As I anticipated this was difficult at first because of its immediate association with romance, boy friends/girl friends etc., but when we had worked through this and moved on to the way you treat and regard friends then things became much easier. Discussion, which was now much more relaxed because it was arising from first-hand experience, brought out a number of points — you must not split on your mates, you'd share

Teaching About Jesus

things with them, you'd stand by them in a fight. They'd do the same for you. There was no shortage of examples, some of which I would have preferred not to have heard! So here we had, from the children themselves, the notion of loving your neighbour as yourself!

The next step could be more difficult. How do you define 'neighbour'? So we talked about perceptions of 'neighbours'. 'Next door neighbour' was seen to be too narrow a definition; in the end it seemed that the term 'neighbour' seemed to be synonymous with 'friend' and 'family'.

In order to move beyond this to develop a more inclusive notion of neighbour, I told the story of the Good Samaritan with some background on the Samaritans and the Jews preceding it. Unfortunately, but not unexpectedly, most of the children had heard the story *many, many,* times before and it had lost its freshness for them! I therefore asked them to write it in their own terms, not talking about Samaritans and Jews but telling it in the way Jesus might have done had he been a current resident in South London. This was a little more exciting but I must say that in general the results were rather disappointing but there was one exception. Alvin, who was generally very quiet and self contained in class, wrote a story which did make the same point in answer to the question 'and who is my neighbour?' Technically the quality was poor so I have put it into normal English:

> There was a Front (National Front) rally in Tower Hamlets. A man who was speaking left. He put some leaflets in his pocket. They were sticking out so you could see them. He was walking down a street by some factories. He met some students who were anti-racists. They saw the leaflets in his pocket. They beat him up and tore up the leaflets. The man was lying on the ground. A bit later another man came along. He was a Front man too. He saw the beaten up man and he saw the torn up leaflets. He was frightened so he ran home. A bit later a black man called Alvin came along. He was driving a big car. He stopped. He saw the leaflets. He put the man who was still unconscious on his back seat. He drove him to the hospital. He rang the man's wife. Then he waited in the hospital 'till she came. Then he went home.

I read this out to the class and opened up discussion. The change was dramatic. 'He was mad!. The Front hates blacks'. 'Should have left him there'. Only very gradually and only from a few children did ideas come that some human concerns are deeper than any ideology. ('He might have died if he'd left him in the road') or that acts like this might in a gradual way begin to change attitudes ('That Front man couldn't be so anti-black after that').

I found the topic stimulating and challenging. I don't know how successful it was and I don't really know how you judge success in any area like this. I think that it made some of the children think about their attitudes. I think too that in areas like this, areas of attitude change, it is like water dripping on a stone. Any change will be very slow and very gradual.

15 An Extended Topic: The Dead Sea Scrolls and Masada

Masada

Studying the fortress of Masada, set on top of a rocky massif to the southwest of the Dead Sea, fulfils two potential roles in religious education. Firstly the story of the Zealots' last stand at Masada against the Romans in AD 73 is dramatic and moving, characterized as it is by extreme courage and single-mindedness and raises many questions among thoughtful people, including children, about the nature of religious commitment. Secondly, it reflects in a very vivid way the type of social and political conditions which provide the backcloth to the life and ministry of Jesus and to the gospels. In the story of Masada, we encounter Herod the Great with his luxurious Roman ways and we meet the Zealots, that group of Jews who felt it was their vocation to expell the Romans from Jewish soil by force. We learn about them through the writings of the Jewish (but pro-Roman) historian, Josephus, and through the findings of archaeology.

The rock of Masada is a natural fortress dropping sheerly on all sides 1300 feet to the Dead Sea. In ancient times there was only one way up to it, by a narrow and tortuous path, called the snake path because of its visual appearance. According to Josephus, the historian, the first to fortify Masada was Jonathan, the High Priest. However, little else is known of this so the story really begins with Herod the Great (died 4 BC).

Herod the Great, perhaps best known to history for his massacre of the young boys in Bethlehem (Matthew, chapter 2, verses 16–18), was half Jewish and King of Judaea by Roman appointment. He was himself a great Romanizer and around the land hippodromes, amphitheatres and other marks of Roman civilization began to appear. The port of Caesarea was a Roman city. Perhaps Herod's greatest achievement was the rebuilding of the temple in Jerusalem.

Herod fortified Masada very thoroughly. Josephus tells us that he did it out of a twofold fear: fear of his own subjects and fear of Cleopatra, Queen of Egypt. Excavations have shown the strength of the walls and the fortifications, the great thought given to the storage of food and water and the opulence of the buildings. This indicates that this was not merely a fortress in Herod's chain of defence but a royal bolt hole, sufficient to maintain him for a long time, if necessary, in the manner in which he was accustomed to live.

Herod's fortress contained among many things palaces, baths, storehouses, villas and a swimming pool. Two of the palaces were clearly Herod's own. The larger, the western palace, was clearly *the* palace of Herod where he had his throne room. It is decorated sumptuously with coloured plastered walls and mosaic floors. In the palace storehouses, there are the broken remains of hundreds of jars and it is possible to read the inscriptions of their contents: 'pressed figs', 'dried figs' and so on. Splendid though the western palace is, it does not compare with the smaller northern palace. This palace, often called the *hanging palace*, is a remarkable feat of engineering. It is perched on the northern nose of the rock and its three levels hang down the rock. From its size it is clear that this palace was a private retreat for Herod and perhaps for one of his wives. It was beautifully positioned, with its rooms and terraces and its hidden staircases, not only for its views but also for climate. Facing north and below the summit of the rock it was free of both the hot sun and the south-west wind. There were also five other smaller palaces or villas no doubt for Herod's wives or for close members of his family. The fortress was well serviced with baths in the Roman style, with cold, tepid and hot water pools and there was an outdoor swimming pool.

An interesting feature in the fortress was the thought given to the problem of withstanding a long seige. Storehouses for food there were in plenty but the real problem on a great rock without a natural spring and set in a desert was *water*. Here Herod's planning was brilliant. Rain does not fall often in that desert but when it does it is violent and torrential. Herod had massive cisterns constructed in the rock, holding in all 1,400,000 cubic feet of water. Close by to Masada are two wadis (that is, dry stream beds which fill with water only during rain). Both of these were damned so that when the rain fell and the wadis gushed with water, the dams created pools which caused the water to run along an elaborate series of aqueducts into the cisterns. Water from the lower cisterns was then taken up to smaller higher cisterns, but this time laboriously by hand.

From Josephus we know that after Herod's death, Masada was

An Extended Topic: The Dead Sea Scrolls and Masada

garrisoned by Roman legionaries until AD 66 when it was captured by a group of Jewish rebels under Menahem. This was part of a country-wide Jewish revolt against Roman power which lasted for four years until AD 70 when the Roman general, Titus, all patience gone, captured Jerusalem, destroyed the city and temple and drove the Jewish survivors away. Judaea was no more. Some of those Zealots who survived the fall of Jerusalem made their way down to join those who held Masada and together they held out against the Romans. Masada was used as a safe place of refuge from which the rebels would sally forth to attack the Roman forces. In AD 72 the decision was taken by the Roman authorities to eliminate the stronghold. The Roman governor, Flavius Silva, marched with the tenth legion to Masada. To attack it was impossible; the only course of action was to lay seige. The 960 inhabitants, men, women and children, under their leader Eleazor prepared for the long battle by rationing food and water. Silva had a wall erected, more than 3000 metres long and two metres thick, which surrounded Masada completely and established eight camps. Masada was now sealed off and the possibility of escape for the Zealots eliminated. It was impossible to scale the sides of the rock so Silva ordered the construction of a ramp on the western side. This was a tremendous undertaking as the ramp was about 200 metres long and began about seventy metres from the wall. In order to stop the ramp collapsing, timber slats were used and the remains of these can still be seen. On top of this ramp, according to Josephus, a large wooden platform was constructed supporting a seige tower with catapults and a battering ram. The missiles from the catapults which are stones the size of grapefruits have been found on the surface of Masada. The battering ram made a breach in the walls but the defenders quickly filled the gaps with a timber replacement which was sufficiently pliable to resist the blows of the battering ram. Silva ordered that the timber wall should be fired and so the breach in the fortress walls was reopened.

This paves the way for the dramatic end of the story. When Eleazor, the Zealot leader, surveyed the damage that evening he knew that the next day the fortress would fall into the hands of the Romans. Rather than be taken prisoner he resolved on another plan. He summoned together the bravest of his companions and put to them the alternative to becoming slaves to the Romans. He proposed that each man should kill his wife and children and then should kill himself. The plan shocked many but Eleazor in a long speech persuaded them to his course of action. Accordingly each man went off, and tenderly bade farewell to his family before killing them. Then ten men were chosen by lot to see to the execution of the men. Then the last remaining man set fire to the palace which contained them before running himself through. Of the defenders of Masada only seven escaped; an old woman, another woman and five children. They hid in caverns and it was they who told the Romans when they occupied the fortress in the morning of the events of the night. The Romans were shocked at the spectacle and amazed at the extent of the courage, patriotism, faith and pride of the defenders. It is quite easy to see how it has become such an evocative story for the modern state of Israel.

The Dead Sea Scrolls

In the spring of 1947, a Bedouin boy, Mohammed the Wolf, was tending his father's goats in the remote and little visited area to the west of the Dead Sea. The limestone cliff face which rises from the plain of the Dead Sea, is honeycombed with caves and it was into one of these that Mohammed the Wolf accidentally threw a stone while he was searching for a wandering goat. The noise the stone made when it fell to the ground was that of breaking pottery! Afraid, the boy did not enter the cave alone but returned with a friend and together they explored the cave.

Inside the two Bedouin boys found several tall, thin clay jars, about four feet high, topped with bowl-like lids. Around these too were the fragments of other broken jars. Inside the jars they found black objects which on investigation turned out to be long rolls of manuscript wrapped in lengths of linen and covered over with a pitch like substance. When unrolled the scrolls were long manuscripts, inscribed in parallel columns on sheets which were sewn together. The boys did not recognize the lettering: in fact it was Hebrew. The boys belonged to a party of contrabanders who were smuggling goods into Palestine to sell on the black market in Bethlehem and it was here that they first tried to sell the scrolls.

The story of how the existence of the scrolls became known both in archaeological circles and to the general public is long and involved and considerably hampered by the hostility between Jews and Arabs at the time. The cave which had contained the scrolls was identified and in 1948 searched. Early in 1952 a five-mile stretch of the cliffs round it was scrutinized and twenty-seven caves were identified of which two contained further manuscript material and twenty-five showed signs of use or habitation from that period. In the next four years, further caves were found which yielded documents. Other caves further away were also discovered containing manuscripts but the most important came from the caves around Qumran.

An Extended Topic: The Dead Sea Scrolls and Masada

Qumran

On a low plateau above the western shore of the Dead Sea and just over half a mile from the cave where the first scrolls were found by Mohammed the Wolf stand the ruins of Khirbet Qumran. Because of its position close to the discovery of the scrolls it was excavated completely over five seasons of digging.

The Qumran buildings comprise several storerooms, a kitchen, a refectory-cum-meeting hall, another room for assembly, and workshops. A particularly interesting find in the ruins was of a large table made out of brick which had fallen through from an upper storey. This contained three inkwells each with dried ink inside and clearly was the centre of a scriptorium where some at least of the manuscripts had been copied.

Around the buildings were places of work: pottery, baking, areas which had been irrigated for cultivation. There were pools of water which would appear to have been baths. Close by to the buildings too is a huge cemetery containing over 1000 graves. The vast majority of the skeletons are male but included among them a few which are female and some of children.

From the excavation of the buildings and from the material in some of the Dead Sea Scrolls it would seem that the community at Qumran was a Jewish religious community, largely celebrate, numbering some several hundred members, most of whom lived in caves or huts by the limestone cliffs. The community building at Qumran provided the centre for eating, for workshop and for common life.

The excavation of the building along with the record of Josephus has enabled its history to be interpreted. It seems that the buildings at Qumran were occupied first about 100 BC and then continuously until 31 BC when there was a severe earthquake. Josephus tells us that 30,000 people in Judaea died in it and that it was particularly severe around Jericho. This is consonant with the buildings at Qumran where there are tremendous cracks evident and it is clear that the rooms fell in on themselves. It appears that it was reoccupied again around the time of the birth of Christ and that the buildings were both restored and modified.

It would seem that the buildings were destroyed by the Romans in AD 68. In the view of Roland de Vaux, the principal archaeologist of the scrolls, Vespasian's tenth legion marched from Caesarea, took Jericho and established a garrison there. From there he pushed on down towards the Dead Sea. Josephus adds the information that Vespasian was curious to see the Dead Sea and to test whether its waters were as buoyant as reports had it. Accordingly he took a number of his men who were non-swimmers and with hands tied behind their backs, had them thrown into the sea. Fortunately they all floated. It seems that Qumran was taken at this time, and that the inhabitants either fled or were killed. Signs of burning and Roman arrow heads were uncovered. Pere de Vaux is of the opinion that the Dead Sea Scrolls were the library of the Qumran community and that it was hidden or left in the caves by members of the community as the Roman army advanced upon them. Thereafter the scrolls were left and forgotten until Mohammed the Wolf's chance stone brought them to light after almost 1900 years.

The Significance of the Scrolls

The Scrolls, well over 600 in number, range from fragments to almost complete documents. Only one, the Isaiah Scroll from the first cave, is complete. Of the manuscripts roughly a quarter are biblical and contain all the books of the Old Testament with the exception of the Book of Esther. There are also copies of two books from the Apocrapha, Tobit and Ben Sirah.

The rest of the manuscripts are collections of quotations, hymns, commentaries on books of the Bible and on theologies. Two important texts, the Rule and the Damascus Document give many clues to the life of the Qumran community and there is also a curious copper scoll.

The Old Testament Texts

What is truly remarkable here is that the caves revealed texts of all the Books of the Hebrew Bible, except for Esther — all dating from the first century AD and in Hebrew. Prior to these discoveries the earliest Hebrew texts of the Old Testament date from the *eleventh century AD!* The older texts raised a number of points for Old Testament scholars but only of a minor nature. The changes in the transmission of the Old Testament texts had been minimal.

The Community

A careful reading of the Scrolls gives a picture, though not a completely clear one, of the community at Qumran.

It was clearly a monastic community, almost exclusively male,

An Extended Topic: The Dead Sea Scrolls and Masada

living under a clear and firm rule of life. The community saw itself as a pious, devout defender of strict Judaism — not the 'corrupt' Judaism that was practiced in Jerusalem. The manuscripts talk of a teacher of righteousness who taught the true way of God and had special insight in the understanding of the scriptures.

In his lifetime he suffered persecution from the Wicked Priest, who belonged to what was seen as the semi-pagan Judaism of the capital. Those who wished to separate themselves from all this could join themselves to the community though entry was difficult — two periods of noviciate were required and faithlessness could well be punished by expulsion. To enter, a postulant had to renounce property and to hold to a life of poverty and hard work. Privilege of membership included participation in community meals and prayers and the careful study of the Jewish law.

There was an underlying assumption that the members of the community and others like it, if there were any, were the only ones left faithful to God. As such they were the 'Sons of Light' in opposition to, and automatically at war with, the 'Sons of Darkness'. If they remained faithful God would in the end reward them.

Some scholars are prepared to indentify the community at Qumran with the Jewish sect 'The Essenes' though many, while noting similarity, are not prepared to do so.

The Copper Scroll

The Copper Scroll found in cave 3 is the only one of the scrolls not on a religious subject and the only one written on copper, an expensive metal, as opposed to papyrus or leather. Because the copper was so heavily oxydized it was impossible to unroll the scroll without it crumbling away. It took four years to discover the contents of the scroll. Then it was opened by cutting it into long narrow strips, rather like children unroll a slice of swiss roll.

The puzzling thing about the scroll is that it tells of the existence of treasure hidden in various parts of the countryside. Large amounts of gold and silver are referred to hidden in places which have a vague quality about them. In all over sixty places are mentioned and they are close to tombs, cisterns, pits and so on.

Great mystery surrounds these entries on the copper scroll. Was it really a treasure or was it symbolic? Some scholars see the contents of the scroll as in some way romantic, though those who disagree point to the fact that the information about the treasure was inscribed upon copper, an expensive metal, which (presumably) had been used because it was likely to last. If it does refer to a treasure whose treasure was it? Did it belong to the community at Qumran or was it the treasure from the temple in Jerusalem which might have been hidden just before the Roman army took Jerusalem.

Masada and the Dead Sea Scrolls in the Classroom

Masada

There can be no doubt that the story of Masada both in the time of King Herod and also during the period of Zealot occupation is both exciting and compelling to children, certainly to those older than eight or nine.

Firstly there is the fascination of discovering how people lived in time past. Secondly there is the dramatic and awesome story of the Roman seige and the resistance by the Zealots.

There are many ways in which imaginative and resourseful teachers can use this story. Two new approaches seem to present themselves.

(i) as an investigation into life in Palestine contemporary with the ministry of Jesus so as to provide a backcloth to the Gospels;
(ii) (a more affective approach) to discuss *why* the Zealots acted as they did.

Here is a record of a project on Masada organized by a teacher with 10/11-year-old children:

> I became interested myself in the story of Masada because I came across Yadin's beautiful book on it. The photography, the text and the dramatic history together were extremely powerful and I felt that there was much in it that would both appeal and be of value to the children in my class. I had already done some work with the children drawing on materials from a variety of religions and this had been successful but I wanted to do some work which would extend their understanding of the Bible as I felt that here there was a neglected area. I knew that there was a resistance on the part of some because their previous experience of Bible work had been of rather 'devout' stories told in a pious and dry way. I hoped that the

An Extended Topic: The Dead Sea Scrolls and Masada

approach through Masada would be different, fresh and appealing. It was very convenient too that during the previous term we had been looking at the work of the archaeologist — there was a dig in the locality and the children had made a visit for an afternoon.

My initial aim at the beginning was fairly limited. I hoped that through this work which was a study, mainly through archaeology, of some aspects of life in Palestine around the time of Jesus that the children would see Jesus and his teaching in a real, human world. I did also hope that it might go beyond this but only time would tell.

My two main tools at the beginning were my copy of Yadin's book and a copy of Josephus' *History of the Jewish People* which I borrowed without any difficulty from the public library. I also collected together a number of books suitable for the children's use which gave information about life at the time of Jesus.

The work began in a 'teacher-centred' way. I began talking to the children about King Herod. What does anybody know about King Herod? He's the one who killed the baby boys in Bethlehem. Horrible man! And so on. So over a period of time we worked through the story from Herod's building of his palace fortress to its destruction by the Romans. I introduced some of the archaeological findings and read extracts from Josephus. The stories had the same power over the children as they had had over me! Tremendous interest was evoked in many different aspects of the project.

It was part of my general strategy with the class to encourage more independence in work so we agreed as a class to establish working groups which would investigate different aspects of the topic, according to special interest. The areas agreed upon were:

(i) Herod's work at Masada in making it into such a secure fortress, with special reference to his water cisterns;

(ii) a reconstruction of the life style of King Herod and his court using the findings of the archaeologists (i.e. the life of the wealthy);

(iii) a reconstruction of the life style of the Zealots using the findings of the archaeologists (i.e. the life style of the ordinary citizen);

(iv) what it was like to live under Roman occupation;

(v) a detailed study of what actually happened in Palestine

around AD 70 using archaeological findings and Josephus' account;

(vi) a study of life at the Qumran monastery with reference to the Dead Sea Scrolls.

Children opted for the area they wished to work on and they divided up fairly well with five or six in each group. The method of working was 'research based' (or research appropriate to the age!). The children began by asking questions and attempting to find answers and then asking further questions. The first group, for example, so fascinated by Herod's amazing water collecting methods, soon found that they were seeking information about conditions of life in the desert. This was supplied by further books from the school library and from the public library. The group investigating life in Palestine under Roman occupation contained a girl who had a French grandmother, now living locally, who had been in France as a young woman during the wartime German occupation. She was able to talk about her experiences there and this enabled the children to see much more clearly beyond the *facts* of the Roman occupation to the feelings of the Jews who were occupied.

The children worked in this way and they recorded their findings in writing, painting and even drama. My role as teacher was partly as a resource, pointing to possible sources of information. It was also as a questioner: where are you going to go from here? how about this? It also involved seeing that the children were working efficiently and effectively. It has always been my view that children who are interested and involved in their work will produce work of a higher standard in every way and this project bore this out.

When I came to evaluate the work at the end, there was no doubt that as a *method* of working it had been very successful. The children had the satisfaction of knowing that they had worked successfully in a cooperative way and had used their initiative effectively. The work produced was almost universally of a high standard and was very varied in its scope and type.

As far as 'religious education' was concerned I was very pleasantly surprised. My fairly limited aim of hoping that the children would, through the work, come to see the world of that time as a real, human world was certainly fulfilled and it came in odd ways. It hit one girl very suddenly when she saw a photograph of a bracelet found at Masada not unlike one of her own. 'Do you mean there were girls there who liked pretty jewellery?'!

An Extended Topic: The Dead Sea Scrolls and Masada

Beyond this there were two significant extensions.

Firstly, the group investigating Herod's water cisterns came up with the interesting comment that they now saw what Jesus meant when he said that he was the living water. Their study of a dry climate had shown them the significance of water and, therefore, prepared them for this symbolic language.

Secondly, many children began to ask questions along the lines of 'How could people (i.e. the Romans) treat other people (i.e. the Jews) like that?' and 'How could people prefer to die rather than to be captured?' This fuelled many discussions and I became aware that children were begining to understand another aspect of religion: that it was more than beliefs, festivals and rituals but involved enormous levels of feeling, loyalty and conviction.

Here is another account by a teacher of 8–9 year old children this time of a topic she did on the *Dead Sea Scrolls*.

Many years ago I had heard the story of the young Bedouin goatherd throwing his stone to frighten his straying goat down the cliffs near the Dead Sea and of the amazing discovery which he accidentally made. I have often told this story to children, as a story in its own right, and they have always found it exciting.

This year, with my 8–9-nine-year-old children, I felt that we ought in RE to do some work on how the Bible came to us, with particular reference to how it was written down and transmitted. I was not at this age and stage concerned with questions of editorship or who decided what ought to be written but how the text was actually written down. I also wanted to link this with archaeology — how we actually know about this.

It seemed to me that a very good approach was by looking at the Dead Sea Scrolls. Here we have the scrolls themselves hidden away in these caves, in the tall jars. We have the monastery at Qumran which included within it the remains of a scriptorium where scrolls were copied down — even with the remains of the dried ink in the inkwells!

This is how it developed:

1. Basically I began by taking the story of Mohammed the Wolf and using this as a means of setting the scene in a colourful way: the pale blue of the Dead Sea, the parched ground, the great heat, the limestone cliffs

with their hundreds of caves and the community living in their monastery at Qumran.

2   Then we asked the question of how we knew how the community had lived. This resulted in much discussion but it refined down to what we could find out from archaeology and secondly, from any written source, if one existed.

3   We began to concentrate first of all on the archaeological evidence. I had ready various accounts and transcribed various extracts on to cards for the children to read. These dealt with such matters as:
(a) inhabited caves;
(b) water channels and cisterns;
(c) the potters' workshop;
(d) the various rooms which have been uncovered;
(e) the scriptorium and the inkwells;
(f) the cemetery and the skeletons.

In this way by gathering the data the children were encouraged to try to interpret it and so to try to construct a picture of the life of the community.

4   With the more able of the pupils, I also did some work on dating, using information about coins found and quotations from Josephus concerning the earthquake of 31 BC.

5   After the children had constructed their own picture I produced extracts from the 'Community Rule' and the 'Damascus Rule'. (I found a copy of G. Vermes' book *The Dead Sea Scrolls in English* in the library) and so the children were able to compare their interpreted picture from the archaeological finds with the accounts in the manuscripts.

6   We then began to focus upon the work of the scribes in the community; the copying of the documents and the care taken of them. What were the scrolls made of? How was leather prepared? How was papyrus made? Why were important documents transcribed in this way?

7   We found out more of how the Dead Sea Scrolls were preserved in the caves and something of the work of scholars in piecing them together and translating them.

8   Naturally a high spot of the project was to make our own scrolls, copying in actual Hebrew script!

An Extended Topic: The Dead Sea Scrolls and Masada

I think that the work was quite demanding of the children. First of all, the method encouraged the children not to rely upon being told the information but to try to deduce it for themselves using the evidence provided. It certainly gave them first hand experience of historical method. If anything, this was, in retrospect, the most valuable part of the project for the children. In addition I think it gave them a new insight into how the Bible came to be formed.

I think that I would like to do further work with the children in two areas: more use of archaeology in reconstructing life as a background to the story of Jesus and a more extended look at the transmission of the Bible, and perhaps of other sacred books as well.

16 Belief in Action

In chapter 4 religion was presented as a six-dimensional activity in which all the six dimensions — doctrinal, mythological, ethical, ritual, experiential, social — represent essential aspects of religion, all of which are interrelated. In helping younger children to understand religion teachers naturally concentrate heavily upon the mythological and ritual dimensions because these are most appropriate to the age and stage of the children. Two of the dimensions, the ethical and the social, together present an important area of religious understanding, often neglected in schools, which is the relationship of the religious adherent to the world at large. Religion does not just take in the sanctuary, believers live in the world, in some places a hostile world, and live out their religion there.

There are two different aspects to this.

Firstly, all religions lay upon their followers certain ethical rules or principles which should govern their conduct or behaviour. Examples of these are the Ten Commandments in Judaism and the Law of Love in Christianity. It is everyday experience that believers fail to live up to these ethical requirements! Many of the rules or principles regulate one individual's behaviour towards another. In the Ten Commandments, for example, there are injunctions against stealing, bearing false witness, committing adultery and so on. The ethical dimension of religions stress such matters as caring for the poor or helping those in need. In Judaism, for example, there is great concern for the 'stranger within the gate', in Islam there is the great tradition of hospitality to strangers and also zakat, the tax for the poor.

Secondly, religions do have within themselves a vision of how the world ought to be and convictions about the relationship of human being with human being and human being with the world at large. Islam, for example, has the noble vision of the 'Brotherhood of Man'.

Belief in Action

The Judaeo-Christian tradition has a great vision of mankind made in the image of God and all men and women as brothers and sisters and children of the same God. During some periods of history these visions are ignored or forgotten; at other times, they assert themselves. William Wilberforce's work in the eighteenth century towards ending slavery in the British Empire is an example of this religious vision: that the Christian view of the human race as all children of God precluded some from owning others. This same vision has spurred others on to work for the relief of poverty, hunger and suffering and for the creation of just and free societies. In very recent times it has led to great concern for matters of conservation: if this is God's world which he has entrusted to us, it is argued, then we should be good stewards and not exploit it for short term gain.

This is an area of controversy. There are many, both within religious communities and without who draw a clear line between the *sacred* and the *secular*, and argue that the only proper sphere of activity for religions is the sacred. This usually means that religions should concern themselves solely with what is often called the 'spiritual' (worship, prayer, teaching about God etc.) and with personal morality. Many others would reject this as too narrow a view. It seems likely to remain an area of permanent debate and disagreement.

If it is the teacher's concern to help children to understand religions as *living* activities, then, as well as looking at, say, festivals, it is very important to consider both the ethical demands laid upon believers and the relationship of religions to the societies in which they are set.

Much of this work will be suited to the older children in the age group, namely to the 10, 11 and 12-year-olds because the younger ones will have insufficient experience to understand the issues at stake. It may well be that there are some stories which would be suitable for younger children, but in general the focus of the work will be directed to the older children.

Two approaches will be considered: through individual case studies and through a project on planning the ideal community.

Individual Case Studies

A significant aspect of religious education has always been the individual case study or biography. Rather than, say, talking in general terms about Christian principles of loving your neighbour as yourself and about the concern for the poor and the unwanted rooted deep in the Christian tradition, why not tell the story of Mother Teresa? Concrete examples are so much clearer than abstract ideas and certainly far more vivid and they pinpoint the principles in real life. This is the theory behind the use of individual case studies.

All religions have within their traditions people who might be described as 'saints', that is, people who have exemplified in their lives or their actions some qualities which have set them above the general level of adherents and made them to some extent examples or models.

Preliminary Considerations

As there are very many case studies from which to select, a number of factors should be borne in mind:

(a) Be careful of *overusing*. Mother Teresa, for example, is in danger of this fate. The nature of her commitment, the nature of her work and the award to her of the Nobel Peace Prize account for her extreme popularity as a case study, but she is in danger of overexposure. 'Not Mother Teresa again!'.

(b) Select carefully. Dr Schweitzer figured on most teachers' lists of case studies for many, many years because he gave up a dazzling career in order to devote his medical talents to the relief of leprosy in Africa at his hospital at Lambarene. Since then he has fallen from favour because of his alleged racist views and attitudes.

(c) It is important that case studies are drawn from different religious traditions and that this should happen in schools without any children from ethnic minorities as well as in those which are racially mixed. When we are considering the teaching of children up to the age of twelve, it may well be that most of the examples are drawn from the Christian tradition but it would be very sad if there was no mention of the tolerance and understanding of Guru Nanak, the courage of Guru Gobind Singh or the non violent tradition of the Mahatma Ghandi.

(d) Make sure that the children are able to have some understanding of the situation in which the chosen case study was active. If Trevor Huddleston, for example, is taken as a case study then it is essential that children have *some* understanding of apartheid.

(e) If it is at all possible try to use people in the local

community. One teacher discovered that a church in a socially deprived area quite close to her school ran a sheltered workshop for handicapped people. A visit there did much more to assist pupils to see religions in action than lots of case studies from distant places.

Examples

Young Children

The most suitable approach at this stage would be to select a particular quality, for example, courage or caring, and to choose an example which illustrates that quality. To take 'courage', the old favourite example of Grace Darling who risked her own life in rowing out in stormy seas to rescue shipwrecked sailors is as good as any.

To take 'caring for animals' the old story of St Francis is as good as any, though it should be remembered that there is much more to St Francis than that!

In general with younger children it is often better to take examples within the children's own experience. To take caring, for example, it is often more appropriate to look at people within the children's experience — the school nurse, the school crossing officer, the community policeman, the school secretary and so on — and to look at ways in which they demonstrate caring qualities.

With Older Children

The use of case studies with children of 9 years or more can be a very rewarding approach adding both interest and excitement. The stories tend to be heroic in that they represent the subjects making a stand for what they believe to be right, often against a background of great resistance and of great personal cost. Some are comparatively straightforward, others are more complex because of the situation in which they are set.

One type of case study would concentrate on the *possible cost of discipleship*. An excellent example of this is the wartime story of Maximilian Kolbe, a Roman Catholic monk who was imprisoned in a concentration camp because of his religious allegiance. While in there he substituted himself for a Jewish prisoner on the way to the gas chambers because this prisoner had a wife and family. Stories of this sort should speak for themselves as impressive human actions. They will almost certainly provoke discussion and the teacher may well use this opportunity to consider the strength of religious belief.

Another type of case study would concentrate upon the activity of an individual who felt driven by his religious beliefs *to concentrate upon a particular task,* often at personal cost. A popular example of this is Father Damien, the nineteenth-century Beligan mission priest who while working in Hawaii heard of the plight of the lepers in the leper colony on Molokai. He sought permission to go as their priest and against the background of initial hostility from the lepers and indifference from the authorities managed to create a self respecting community — before he himself contracted leprosy and died.

A third type of case study would concentrate upon the activity of an individual who felt compelled by his convictions to resist laws and systems which he felt to be unjust. One example here would be Trevor Huddleston, the Anglican monk sent by his community to work in the large black parish of Sophiatown in South Africa. Here he found that many of the regulations and laws with regard to blacks so offended his conscience that he was compelled to protest on both a national and international scale. Similar case studies would be those of Martin Luther King and Helder Camara. In all these three examples the pupils need to have some understanding of the political and social background.

There are, of course, numerous case studies which could be selected: Mother Teresa, Elizabeth Fry, Lord Shaftesbury, Dr. Barnardo, Mahatma Ghandhi to name but a very few. The great problem is always one of relevance and very often a local person, perhaps far less heroic, can seem more real. A number of series of booklets are now being brought out which try to meet this concern (see 'Resources').

Planning an Ideal Community

A useful way of encouraging children to think about and discuss the practical implications of beliefs for living is to set them the task of planning an ideal community. A teacher of 11-year-olds describes how such an activity worked.

> In my RE work with my class I had been looking at the implications of religious faith for the way life is lived. My method had been the time hallowed one of telling stories of remarkable men and women. In some senses it has all gone

very well. I know I tell stories well and the children have enjoyed them, have been prepared to talk about and seemed to have remembered them. On the other hand, I was not convinced that it has had much personal impact upon the children! I was very puzzled about what to do until I overheard a heated argument between two children. The news had just been leaked to the press of a proposal to close the local cottage hospital on the grounds of cost. One girl was shocked by this while a boy thought it a sensible idea. I joined in the argument and asked the question 'why'. The girl was not very articulate but it became clear that she was worried that if the physiotherapy section closed, it would make life very difficult for many old people. The boy thought that too much money was spent on hospitals. It struck me that this was really an argument about values, about what was really important. That was where the idea began.

The following week I talked to all the children as a class and explained to them that I was going to split them into groups of five and that each group had to plan the ideal town/village. The end product was to be a model of the community showing roads, houses and other buildings. In order to reach that goal, each group would have to sort out (a) what buildings and services ought to be there and (b) where these ought to be placed. I thought the task might daunt the children but it didn't seem to. In fact the groups settled down to it very quickly.

The quality of the discussion, in terms of ideas, in interactive argument and in the language use, was very impressive indeed. There were many discussions on the need for things like hospitals, firestations, dentists, hairdressers, supermarkets, parking, family housing, housing for old people, places of worship, community centres and many, many other things. The next stage was where to place them. Should the community centre be at the centre, or perhaps the church or the supermarket?

In the end seven different village models were produced — in some ways very similar, in others very different. What of course was important was the decision making process that went on during the work with a free discussion of values. I felt that this was a much more constructive approach. Nothing was imposed but the children had been challenged to think and to make decisions on questions of values.

17 Resources

There are many aids to teaching and learning in religious education that resourceful teachers can use successfully. There are the more obvious aids like books, pictures and charts which are multiplying year by year. In addition to these are less-used but potentially highly significant resources such as religious buildings, religious artefacts and, of course, people.

Religious Buildings

All religions express themselves in some form of community and all establish some building or place where ceremonies and worship can be carried out. These buildings where the faithful meet to worship, to celebrate, to hallow the important stages of life and to teach the religion to both young and old have a very special place in the life of that religious community. They contain also the sacred objects of the religion: the Sikh temple houses the throne of the Guru Granth Sahib, the Christian church the altar, the Hindu temple the images of the gods, or more precisely the images of some of the manifestations of God. To try to understand any religion without experiencing its place of worship is an impossibility. To experience it additionally as a *living* centre is infinitely preferable though not always possible in the working week.

All teachers have a fairly easy access to a place of worship. For all there is the possibility of a visit to a church whether it be the village church, the cathedral or the town church on the corner. For some there is the possibility of visiting a mosque or a temple. Places of worship are one of the most important resources available to teachers in the area of religious education — and yet are so often neglected. To fulfil their potential visits need to be carefully planned and organized.

Visiting a Place of Worship

As it is likely that most visits arranged by teachers will be to churches, the discussion here will be concerned principally with these visits.

Purpose

It is possible to describe a place in words and in so doing paint a vivid picture. To support this description with photographs or even with a film can reinforce this strongly. Neither can take the place of the first hand experience of a visit.

Taking children to visit a church probably has two main purposes.

Firstly, an important consideration is that the atmosphere of a church can 'speak' to the feelings. Many people visit churches and say that in some they feel a sense of peace or tranquillity. In others, they have feelings of timelessness or eternity. Visitors to cathedrals like Durham often claim that it speaks to them of majesty and power, others to Chartres of mystery and depth. Some buildings do speak to people at a level other than that of conscious thought and this is an experience which can be very important for children. Often teachers for various organizational reasons have to take children to the nearest church. If there is a choice it may be wise to bear the question of 'atmosphere' in mind.

Secondly, children will be able to see what the interior of a church is like, to see the various artefacts of worship and to identify them. For older children there would be the additional aim of understanding the purpose of these artefacts for those who use the building.

Organization

1 Select the most appropriate church and approach the clergyman or minister to see if a visit is possible.
2 The teacher should make a preliminary visit to ascertain the whereabouts of toilets, of places to eat a packed lunch (if desired) and any places of danger.
3 Ask the clergyman if he can be available during the visit to

Religious Education 5–12

help answer questions or to talk to the children about some of the artefacts, for example the vessels for holy communion or the vestments. If it is possible and the clergyman can communicate well with the children, invite him to come into school before the visit to talk.
4   The visit should be part of the work the children are doing and there should be preparatory work and follow up work.
5   Usually children should be given a worksheet appropriate both to their age and to the work they are doing.
6   Because people are particularly sensitive to behaviour in church, visits need to be carefully planned and supervised. It is a good idea to make sure that visits are not too long and that children are not allowed to climb, for example, upon altars! Often it is useful to break the children into small groups for working.

Possible Activities

1   If the teacher wants the children to see the church as a *used* building, then it is very helpful if the clergy and/or some members of the worshipping congregation are there to talk to the children both as a whole group and informally as they carry out their work. This is always potentially difficult because the members of the congregation present may not be good at communicating with children and the occasion should not be seen as an opportunity to proselytize. Teachers may need to make discreet enquiries beforehand.
2   What the children are asked to do on the visit will depend upon the overall aims of the work they are doing, in which the visit has its place. It may be that the children have been hearing about such items as pulpits, lecterns, pews, altars, fonts and so on and have come to see them in their setting. It may well be that the children have come to the church to see how the various artefacts are used in worship. Whatever the specific purpose of the visit, the activities of the children can be directed towards it.
3   Many teachers complain that activities on such a visit which amount to little more than 'this is a pew' or 'this is a kneeler' can be very boring for children. A number have found that, certainly with younger children, it is best to focus upon a few

items and to develop them. For example, the children's attention could be diverted towards the *font*.

The font: what is it made of? what shape is it? what is it like inside? Ask the clergyman to demonstrate how he performs a baptism at the font. Back at school talk to the children about baptisms/christenings. Ask them to bring in photographs of family baptisms. Discuss christening robes. Ask if any of the children can bring one into school. Discuss the significance of baptism: the giving of *Christian names* and the making of the person a child of God. Talk about baptisms of adults by total immersion. Some teachers may like to look at 'initiation' rites in other religions, for example, among Sikhs or Muslims.

It may be that many children would find such an approach, focussing upon a small number of artefacts like lecterns and candles in this way, much more satisfying than covering a wide range of items more superficially.

Visits to Other Places of Worship

Schools which have the good fortune to be near synagogues, mosques, gurdwaras or temples will want to arrange for their pupils to make visits there. Arranging a visit to one of these places of worship should not differ significantly from arranging one to a church. Some things do need to be borne in mind:

1. Sikhs, Jews, Muslims and Hindus feel at least as strongly as Christians and probably more so about appropriate behaviour in places of worship.
2. Different religious traditions have different ways of showing respect. Jewish, Sikh and Muslim worshippers would normally cover the head when entering a place of worship. Sikhs, Muslims and Hindus take off their shoes at the entrance. Sikhs would expect visitors to make some gesture of respect to the throne of the Guru Granth Sahib, though not necessarily the full obeisance.
3. Visitors will often find that they are the recipients of generosity or hospitality. It is, for example, rare to leave a Hindu temple without receiving some fruit or nuts, themselves originally an offering from a worshipper. In the Gurdwara, visitors will usually be offered *karah parshad* and perhaps taken off to the kitchen area where they may be offered anything from a full curry dish to a cup of (very sweet) tea and a biscuit.

4 It is not unknown for parties of school children to visit places of worship and, finding that the strangeness makes them embarrassed, to giggle and to be generally impolite. If teachers are aware of this possibility then they can guard against it.
5 It is very important that teachers should make a visit themselves in advance of the children's visit so that they know what is likely to happen. This will make the visit a much smoother and more valuable educational experience.

People

It was emphasized in the previous section that the presence of a clergyman on a visit to a church centre is extremely helpful because he is able to explain and to demonstrate. In the same way, the presence of an adherent of a religion in a classroom can, in principle, be very valuable.

A teacher with a class of 10-year-old children had been studying the medieval monastery mainly by visiting the ruins of one only a few hundred yards from the school. The children drew maps of their local priory, identified the church, the refectory, the gatehouse, the dorter and so on and over a peiod began to reconstruct the life of the monastery with its rhythm of work and prayer. The teacher, concerned that the children should not see monasticism just as a medieval eccentricity, began to tell the class about monasticism today. To make this come alive he invited a very personable monk to come to talk to the class about his life in the monastery. The monk was able to pitch his talk to the level of the children who were completely absorbed. In their talk and in the questions that followed it the monk was able to convey not only *what* he did in his life but also something of *why*. In their topic the children had gone beyond mere information into some degree of religious understanding.

The teacher was very fortunate in his choice of monks. Others might well have overestimated the level of the children and so the same results would not have been achieved. An unsuccessful speaker is worse than no speaker at all.

When inviting outside speakers into the classroom teachers need to bear in mind three things.

Firstly, that the speaker should be able to communicate with the children at their own level (and this includes ensuring that in the case of speakers from ethnic minority groups the children should be able to

Resources

understand their speech); secondly, that the speaker's visit should be an integral part of the overall work; and thirdly that the speaker should be thoroughly briefed about the whole topic and about his part within it.

These considerations help to ensure that an outside speaker's visit is worthwhile.

Artefacts

Even though it is not always appropriate to arrange a visit to places of worship for all sorts of reasons, it should always be possible to provide children with first-hand experiences of some of the artefacts associated with different religions. Such artefacts can be borrowed from various resource centres and teachers' centres and in a multiracial area from local people who practice a particular religion and may be prepared to lend objects of interest. It is not impossible for schools or individual teachers to build up their own limited collection of artefacts as they can be bought quite cheaply from shops which supply the needs of the various ethnic minority groups. A teacher who was developing a topic on Islam wanted to focus upon the practice of prayer. He had a wall chart depicting a prayer mat, he got children to design their own prayer mats. The work came to life when he produced a real Muslim prayer mat upon which the children would sit and which had a compass incorporated into it which enabled the worshippers to face Mecca with ease. This was the real thing!

Interest tables which provide appropriate artefacts for children to pour over and to handle almost inevitably motivate children. A teacher had been talking to her class about the five Ks as marks of Sikkhism. The children dutifully learned all this but the work took on new life when the teacher produced an interest table on Sikhisim which as well as including the usual pictures and books also included the five Ks: a picture of an adult male Sikh with loose hair, a bracelet, a pair of shorts, the hair comb and the sword. The children were not only able to see but to touch and feel.

Religion Box

Another approach is through the *Box*. Many teachers have what they call their Christianity Box, their Muslim Box and so on. These are small collections of artefacts highly significant to the religion in question.

Here are two accounts by teachers of their rationale in choosing the five objects:

> 1. When I came to choose five objects for my Christianity Box I began to find difficulties immediately — difficulties, that is, of restricting my choice to five: it seemed obvious that a copy of the Bible should be in the box because of its importance in Christian life and worship and because it is the source of many of the stories about religion. Next I chose a crucifix because this representation of Christ on the cross is so widespread in Christian art and worship and such a focus for prayer and devotion. Then I chose a book of prayers because worship of God is tremendously important in Christianity. Candles are highly symbolic of light and prayer — they burn on altars and they twinkle before statues in churches so I included one of those. Lastly I chose a rosary because its use is widespread, because it is pleasant and attractive to handle and because it emphasizes prayer and worship. Inevitably this is a personal selection but it does represent what *I* see as highly significant in Christianity.

> 2. For me, any collection of Christian artefacts would include a cross because the cross of Jesus lies at the centre of Christianity and it is represented everywhere — in churches, on church spires, in necklaces, in brooches and so on. The New Testament would also be there because it contains the basic documents of the Christian religion — namely the accounts of the life of Jesus and the reflections of the earliest followers. If this could be in a language other than English, then this would be better still as it would emphasize the universal nature of Christianity. For me the holy communion, the eucharist, stands at the centre of Christian life and worship so I would include a wafer as representing this. Saints, too, have always been important in my experience of Christianity so I would include in my box too a small icon of the Virgin Mary or one of the major saints like Peter or Paul. And fifthly and lastly, I would include a printed card of the Lord's Prayer which has been the best known prayer to all Christians in all ages.

These are two specific examples of 'Christianity boxes'. There are many others too. Another teacher with a liking for materials and embroidery and with an eye for colour set up a display of the following items which she took out of her (admittedly large) box: an altar frontal, a priest's chasuble, a confirmation veil, a pascal (Easter) candle and an embroidered kneeler.

These examples have so far been illustrative of Christianity. Jewish boxes, Muslim boxes, Sikh boxes and so on are equally important and often of even greater interest to children because their contents are likely to be less familiar. A Jewish box for example, might include all or any of the following objects: a copy of the Hebrew Bible, a copy of the Ten Commandments, a tallith (a prayer shawl), a yarmulka (skull cap), phyllacteries, mezuzahs, matzoh, candlesticks as used in the ceremonies of the home. Many more artefacts could, of course, be added depending upon the focus of the teaching.

Festivals' Box

An effective way of approaching the teaching of a festival is to select a number of relevant artefacts which serve as concrete objects upon which the background stories and the ceremonies of the festival can be hung. An account by a teacher of 6–7-year-old children on her approach to Easter illustrates this.

> When I was planning my work for the spring term I noticed in my diary that Easter was very early and that term did not end until the Wednesday of Holy Week. This seemed a good opportunity to make an attempt — one which I had often avoided — to tackle Easter and the events which led up to it. This involves a considerable number of stories and I feared that they might become all jumbled up in the children's minds. To try to avoid this I decided to select seven objects upon which I could focus or cluster the stories. The objects which I chose were:
>
> Palm Cross
> Maundy Money
> Hot Cross Bun
> Picture of St. Veronica
> A cross or crucifix
> Easter Egg
> Picture of Mary Magdalene in the garden
>
> I began the work by showing the children a Palm Cross

which one of the class provided. I managed to 'undo' it without tearing it to show that it is in fact one leaf and we talked about palm trees. Nigel, who had brought the Palm Cross, told the class how he had acquired it the previous year which he remembered very clearly because a donkey had been brought into the church. A number of other children too remembered that they had been there as well. At story time the next day I told the story of Jesus' entry into Jerusalem in a dramatic and colourful way.

I had the good fortune to be able to borrow one of the Maundy coins which the Queen distributes on Maundy Thursday together with a picture I had of the occasion. The children had the opportunity to handle the coin and inspect it closely. I talked about the picture and encouraged the children to interpret what was happening. They were able to establish quite a lot of the story from the clues in the picture and I completed the rest. I then explained that originally the monarch used to wash the feet of poor people and I tried to find out from the children why that should be. On a subsequent occasion I told the story about Jesus washing his disciples' feet in the upper room.

It is amazing how early in Lent you can buy hot cross buns in the shops. I bought a few and we also made some in class. Most of the children knew the nursery rhyme *Hot Cross Buns* and from this I told them in a very simple way that on Good Friday Jesus had been put to death on a cross. The horrors of crucifixion was not an issue I wanted to raise or discuss with the children. I had a crucifix on the interest table and I felt that was enough.

I had a photograph of the Stations of the Cross from a modern local church which depicted St. Veronica wiping Jesus' face. I told the children of Jesus' journey carrying his own cross from his trial to Calvary and described the crowd shouting abuse at him as he dragged himself along. Then out of the hostile crowd came a woman who wiped his brow with a cloth upon which his sweat made the impression of his features. The children found the story very moving but some, remembering the warm welcome given to Jesus on Palm Sunday, could not understand the change in the mood of the crowd. This provoked considerable discussion among the children as many had had similar experiences. 'Some days everybody likes you, other days the same people can be very nasty' was the way one child put it.

Although I realize that the Resurrection of Jesus is not accepted as a 'fact' by many people I felt that I could not leave Jesus on the cross. Of the various Resurrection stories in the Bible I chose the one where Mary Magdalene, having found the tomb empty and thinking that Jesus' body has been stolen, begins to search first in the garden. She meets the man who she thinks is the gardener but finds it is Jesus.

We talked too about Easter eggs, both the type made out of chocolate and those which are hard boiled. The teacher in the classroom next door had a small incubator and was hatching out chickens. The children made several visits in groups to see the progress there and there was great excitement when the chicks began to emerge. We talked quite a bit about why we gave eggs at Easter and the experience of seeing the hatchings gave a few of the children a glimmering. We made some Easter eggs ourselves by hard boiling them and then painting them. We also looked at the custom of egg rolling on Easter Day, rolling away the stone from the door of the tomb.

It is always difficult to evaluate work of this kind with young children — in the end you never quite know how they make sense of the stories. However, it seems that by selecting a few stories to tell and then relating them to a number of concrete objects the children seemed to be much more highly motivated in the work and to be able to talk about it with greater interest and understanding than I had noticed previously.

Books

There are many books available which can be of use to anyone teaching RE to children. Below is a *selection* of some which the teacher might find useful. Where the books are for children's use an attempt has been made to indicate appropriate age groups. The principal criterion in this has been the text. However, many of the books are so well illustrated that teachers of much younger children will find them of great use.

The bibliography has been divided into the following sections:

Religious Education 5-12

Classroom books relating to world religions
Classroom books relating to the Bible
Classroom books on biography
Useful books for theme work
Useful background books for teachers on world religions
Useful background books for teachers on the Bible
Useful books on religious education

Classroom Books Relating to World Religions

Until very recently there was a dearth of classroom books for pre-adolescent children on world religions. However the impetus of general concern for a multicultural understanding of society has resulted in a large number of generally high quality books aimed at younger children. Many of these are very suitable for RE work.

Bell and Hyman	**Exploring Religions Series**		10+
	People	)	
	Buildings	)	
	Worship	) O Bennett (1984)	
	Writings	)	
	Festivals	)	
	Signs and Symbols	)	
A & C Black	**Celebrations**		8+
	Dat's New Year (Chinese)	L Smith (1985)	
	Diwali	C Deshpande (1985)	
	New Baby	J Baskerville (1985)	
	Sam's Passover	L Hannigan (1985)	
A & C Black	**Strands**		8+
	Nahda's Family (Muslim)	M Blakeley (1977)	
	Pavan is a Sikh	S Lyle (1977)	
	The Phoenix Bird Chinese Take-away	K Mackinnon (1978)	
	Simon, Leah and Benjamin (Jewish)	C Knapp (1979)	
Franklin Watts	**My Belief Series**		8+
	I Am a Muslim	M Aggarwal (1984)	
	I Am a Hindu	M Aggarwal (1984)	
	I Am a Buddhist	M Aggarwal (1985)	

	I Am a Jew	C Lawton (1984)
	I Am a Sikh	M Aggarwal (1984)
	I Am a Rastafarian	O Robinson (1985)
	I Am a Greek Orthodox	M Rousou (1985)
	I Am a Roman Catholic	B Pattenuzzo (1985)
Ginn & Co	**Celebrations Series**	7+
	Eid-ul-Fitr	K McLeish (1985)
	Diwali	B Candappa (1985)
	Hannukka	L Berg (1985)
	Christmas	L Berg (1985)
	Chinese New Year	K McLeish (1985)
Hamish Hamilton	**The Way We Are Series**	8+
	Kilkar's Drum	O Bennett (1984)
	A Sikh Wedding	O Bennett (1985)
	Colin's Baptism	O Bennett (1986)
	Gifts and Almonds (Muslim)	J Solomon (1980)
	Bobbi's New Year (Sikh)	J Solomon (1980)
	News for Dad (Sikh)	J Solomon (1980)
	A Present for Mum (Hindu)	J Solomon (1981)
	Wedding Day (Hindu)	J Solomon (1981)
	Matza and Bitter Herbs (Jewish)	C Lawton (1984)
	Ananada in Sri Lanka (Buddhist)	C Baker (1984)
Hulton	**Our World: Life and Faith Series** (1983)	7+
	Hinduism	
	Islam	
	Buddhism	
	Judaism	
Lutterworth	**Understanding Your Neighbour Series**	9+
	Understanding Your Jewish Neighbour	M Domnitz (1974)
	Understanding Your Muslim Neighbour	M and M Iqbal (1976)
	Understanding Your Hindu Neighbour	J Ewen (1977)
	Understanding Your Sikh Neighbour	P Singh Samhi (1980)

Religious Education 5–12

Lutterworth	*Visiting an Anglican Church*	S Tomkins (1981)	9+
	Visiting a Community Church	G Palmer (1981)	
	Visiting a Roman Catholic Church	D Sullivan (1981)	
	Visiting a Sikh Temple	D Kaur Babraa (1981)	
Lutterworth	**Thinking About Series**		11+
	Thinking About Islam	J B Taylor (1971)	
	Thinking About Judaism	M Domnitz (1971)	
	Thinking About Hinduism	E J Sharpe (1971)	
	Thinking About Christianity	R St. L Broadberry (1974)	
	Thinking About Buddhism	D Naylor (1976)	
Macdonald	*The Hindu World*	P Bahree (1982)	11+
	The Muslim World	R Tames (1982)	
	The Buddhist World	A Bancroft (1984)	
	The Christian World	A Brown (1984)	
Macmillan Educational	**Festival! Series**		9+
	Ramadan and Eid ul-Fitr)		
	Carnival)	O Bennett (1986)	
	Diwali)		
	Chinese New Year)		
Accompanying Teachers' Notes and Pupils' Worksheets		R Kerven (1986)	
Macmillan Educational	*At Home and Abroad with Amar and Zarqa,* (Two Muslim Children))))		10+
	At Home and Abroad with Amardip and Rema, (Two Sikh Children))))		
	At Home and Abroad with Daksa and Arun, (Two Hindu Children))))	S W Harrison (1986)	
	At Home and Abroad with Ellen and Alan, (Two Barbadian Children))))		

Resources

Oliver and Boyd	**Leaders of Religion Series**	11+

Moses)
Muhammed) Dilwyn Hunt (1985)
Jesus)

Religious and Moral Education Press	**Families and Faiths Series**	10+

A Hindu Family in Britain	P Bridger (1969)
A Jewish Family in Britain	V Barnett (1983)
A Sikh Family in Britain	W O Cole (1973)
A Muslim Family in Britain	S W Harrison and D Shepherd (1979)
A Christian Family in Britain	S W Harrison and D Shepherd (1984)

RMEP	**Living Festival Series**	9+

Festivals of the Buddha	A Bancroft (1983)
Christmas	A Ewens (1982)
Easter	N Fairburn and J Priestley (1982)
Hallowe'en, All Souls and All Saints	A Ewens (1983)
Harvest and Thanksgiving	J Priestley and H Smith (1985)
Holy Week	N Fairburn and J Priestley (1984)
Shrove Tuesday, Ash Wednesday and Mardi Gras	M Davidson (1984)
Divali	H Marsh (1982)
Holi	A Bancroft (1984)
Ramadan and Id-ul-Fitr	J Hannaford (1982)
Chanukkah	L Scholefield (1983)
Passover	L Scholefield (1982)
Shabbat	C Bryan (1983)
Guru Nanak's Birthday	M Davidson (1982)
Chinese New Year	A Bancroft (1984)

Religious Education 5–12

Wayland	**Beliefs and Believers Series**	11+

	Buddhists and Buddhism	M Patrick (1982)
	Christians and Christianity	L F Hobley (1979)
	Hindus and Hinduism	P Mitter and S Mitter (1982)
	Jews and Judaism	L F Hobley (1979)
	Moslems and Islam	L F Hobley (1979)
	Sikhs and Sikhism	S S Kapoor (1982)

Wayland	**Families Around the World Series**	8+
	A Family in India	P O Jacobsen and P S Kristensen (1984)

Wayland	**Festivals Series**	10+
	Christmas	A Blackwood (1984)
	Easter	J Fox (1984)
	Hallowe'en	R May (1984)
	Harvest and Thanksgiving	R Whitlock (1984)
	Buddhist Festivals	J Snelling (1985)
	Hindu Festivals	S Mitter (1985)
	Jewish Festivals	R Turner (1985)
	Muslim Festivals	M M Ahson (1985)
	New Year	A Blackwood (1985)
	Sikh Festivals	S S Kapoor (1985)

Wayland	**My Country Series**	8+
for example	*India is My Country*	C and B Moon (1983)

Wayland	**Religions of the World Series**	10+
	Christianity	(1985)
	Hinduism	(1985)
	Islam	(1985)
	Judaism	(1985)

Boyce, R W (1972) *The Story of Islam*, RMEP   11+
Cole, W O and Sambhi, P S (1980) *Meeting Sikhs*, Longmans   11+
Collinson, C and Miller, C (1981) *Believers*, E Arnold   11+
Collinson, C and Miller, C (1984) *Milestones*, E Arnold   11+
El-Droubie, R and Hulmes, E (1980) *Islam*, Longmans   11+
Gray, I and McFarlan, D M (1982) *The Founders' File*, Blackie   11+
Iqbal, M (1980) *Call from the Minaret*, Hodder and Stoughton   11+

Palmer, M and Bisset, E (1985) *Worlds of Difference*, Blackie 11+
Roadley, K P (1977) *Questing: Symbol in World Religions*, 11+
 E Arnold
Roadley, K P (1980) *Your Way and Mine*, E Arnold 11+
Robinson A (1980a) *Mohammed and the Heroes of Islam*,
 Schofield and Sims Ltd
Robinson, A (1980b) *The Jewish Faith and its Heroes*, Schofield 10+
 and Sims Ltd
Thorley, S (1983) *Islam in Words and Pictures*, RMEP 9+
Triggs, T (1981) *Founders of Religions: The Buddha, Jesus* 9+
 Christ and Mohammed, Wayland

Some stories for juniors
Chowdhury, B R (1977) *The Story of Krishna*, Hemkunt Press, New Delhi
Chowdhury, B R (1967) *The Story of Mahabharata*, Hemkunt Press, New Delhi
Landaw, J (1978) *The Story of Buddha*, Hemkunt Press, New Delhi
Mala Singh S (1967) *The Story of Guru Nanak*, Hamkunt Press, New Delhi
Ramachandran, A (1979) *Hanuman*, A & C Black
Thompson, B (1980) *The Story of Prince Rama*, Kestrel Books

Classroom Books Relating to the Bible

Bull, N J (1980) *The Story of Jesus*, Hamlyn 9+
Chichester Project, Lutterworth
  Curtis P (1984) *Exploring the Bible* 11+
  Shannon T (1982) *Jesus* 10+
Connolly P (1983) *Living in the Time of Jesus of Nazareth*, OUP
Denholm House Press **Getting to Know About series** (1975–77) 8+
        A series about life in Bible times:
          1 *Houses and Homes*
          2 *Clothes*
          3 *Food*
          4 *Learning and Playing*
          5 *Animals and Birds*
          6 *Trading and Transport*
          7 *Farming and Fishing*
          8 *The Countryside*
          9 *Places of Worship*

Religious Education 5–12

    10 *People*
    11 *Festivals*
    12 *Roman Life and Customs*
Doney M (1985) *How Our Bible Came to Us*, Lion   10+
Lutterworth, *Stories of Bible Times*, A Farncombe (1977–78)   6–8

    Danny's Picnic; *Sarah and the Search*; *Philip Visits the Temple*; *Reuben and the Olive Harvest*; *Matthew's Day with the Sheep*; *Hannah's Market Day*; *Ben, the Fisherman's Son*; *Seth Goes to School*.   6–9

Ladybird
A number of titles for example, about Jesus:
    Jesus the Helper; *Jesus the Friend*; *Jesus by the Sea of Galilee*; *Jesus Calls his Disciples*.
About Biblical figures:
    The Child of the Temple (Samuel); *The Shepherd Boy of Bethlehem* (David); *The Story of Joseph*; *Moses, Prince and Shepherd*; *The Story of Daniel*; *Naaman and the Little Maid*; *The Story of St. Paul*; *Peter the Fisherman*.

McFarlan, D M and Gray, I S S (1978) *The Nazarene File*, Blackie   10+
Mullen, P and Pitts, M (1979) *Jesus, History in Pictures*, E Arnold   10+
Mullen, P and Pitts, M (1979) *The Apostles — Their Story in Pictures* E Arnold   10+
Priestley J G (1984) *Bible Stories for Today*; RMEP   8+
    1 *The Old Testament*
    2 *The New Testament*
Whanslow, H W (1957) *Paper Reeds and Iron Pens*, RMEP

Classroom Books Relating to Biography

Bull, N J (1973) *One Hundred Great Lives*, Hulton
Hamish Hamilton   **Profiles Series**   9+

Edith Cavell	Richardson N (1985)
Anne Frank	Bull A (1984)
Basil Hume	Noel G (1984)
Helen Keller	Sloan C (1984)
Pope John Paul II	Craig M (1982)
Mother Teresa	Craig M (1983)

E Arnold *People of Courage and Concern*, Horton, RH (1979) 10+
Hulton **Great Christians Series** 9+
    1 *The Early Saints*   )
    2 *New Life in the Church*   )
    3 *Workers for God*   ) N J Bull (1972)
    4 *The Church in all the World*)

Ladybird Books Such titles as: *Florence Nightingale, Joan of Ark, The Pilgrim Fathers, Elizabeth Fry and John Wesley*. 8+

RMEP, **Faith in Action Series** 9+
    There is a large number of titles in this series, for example:

A Man with a Vision (John Groom)	N Martin
A Modern St. Francis (Brother Douglas)	N J Bull
No Compromise (Dietrich Bonhoeffer)	A Constant
City of Darkness (Jackie Pullinger)	G Hanks
Down Among the Dead Men (Sally Trench)	B Peachment
Free at Last (Martin Luther King)	R J Owen
In the Streets of Calcutta (Mother Teresa)	A Constant
Island of No Return (Father Damien)	G Hanks
I Wish He was Black (Trevor Huddleston)	R J Owen

Robinson, A (1980) *The Heroes of Christianity*, Schofield and Sims, Huddersfield 9+

SCM Press **People with a Purpose Series** 10+

1 *Mother Teresa*	S M Hobden (1973)
2 *Trevor Huddleston*	I H Birnie (1973)
3 *Helder Camara*	N Cheetham (1973)
4 *George Macleod*	S M Hobden (1973)
5 *Kenneth Kaunda*	R Trudgian (1973)
6 *Barbara Ward*	N Cheetham and C King (1974)
7 *James Baldwin*	D Edwards and I H Birnie (1975)
8 *Danilo Dolci*	J Ferguson (1975)

Wayland **Great Lives Series** 10+
There is a wide range of lives covered in this series of which some would be very suitable for RE, for example: *Anne Frank*
                                      Helen Keller
                                      Martin Luther King
                                      Mother Teresa
Some books listed in other sections would also be appropriate here.

Useful Books for Theme Work

There are a tremendous number of books available for children from 5 onwards which teachers can use imaginatively. Below are some examples:

Bell and Hyman	**Arjuna's Family Series**	7+
	The Festival) Peter Bonnici (1984)	
	The First Rains)	
A and C Black	**Beans Series**	7+
	For example: *French Family; Apache Family; Singapore Family; Fairground Family; Mexico; Sri Lanka; Sakin in India; Yik Ming in Hong Kong; Bakery; Pottery; The Blacksmith's House.*	
Evans Brothers	**Jafta's Family Series**	7+
	Jafta Hugh Lewin (1981–83)	
	Jafta — My Mother	
	Jafta — My Father	
	Jafta — The Wedding	
	Jafta — The Journey	
	Jafta — The Town	
Franklin Watts	**People Series** For example:	7+
	Dentist S Pepper (1985)	
	Dairy Farmer S Pepper (1985)	
	Vet S Pepper (1985)	
Hamish Hamilton	**Cherrystones Series** For example:	7+
	The Farmer; The Nurse; The Policewoman; The Dustman.	
Ladybird Books	**People at Work Series** For example:	7+
	The Fireman; Policeman; Nurse; Farmer; Postman.	
Methuen Children's Books Ltd (1985)	**The Next Door Books**	7+
	Twin Talk Peter C Heaslip	
	Changing Books Peter C Heaslip	
	Home in Bed Peter C Heaslip	
	No School Today Peter C Heaslip	
Young Library	**People Who Help Us Series**	7+
	Mr Kofi is a Doctor	
	Mr Westbrook is a Dustman	
	Mr Martin is a Postman	
	Mr Bourne is a Milkman	
Aliki (1962) *My Hands*, A & C Black		7+
Curry, P (1982)	*Picture Lions*	
	I Can See	

I Can Hear
I Can Touch
I Can Taste and Smell
Patterson, G (1984) *All About Bread*, Andre Deutsch
Snowdon, L (1982) *Children Around the World*, International Picture Library MacMillan Children's Books
Some books listed in other sections would also be appropriate here.

Useful Background Books for Teachers in World Religions

Butler, D G (1980) *Rejoicing In Our Midst: Forty-two Festivals from Nine Religions*, E Arnold
Carey, D and Large, J (1982) *Festivals, Family and Food*, Hawthorn Press
Christian Education Movement (1984) *Exploring a Theme: Journeys*
Cole, W O (Ed) (1981a) *Comparative Religions*, Blandford Press Ltd
Cole, W O (1981b) *Five Religions in the Twentieth Century*, Hulton
Ferguson, J (1976) *Religions of the World: A Study for Everyman* Lutterworth Educational
Hinnells, J R (Ed) (1984) *A Handbook of Living Religions*, Viking
Jones, A A (Ed) (1981) *Illustrated Dictionary of World Religions*, RMEP
Marnham, P (1980) *Lourdes*, Granada
Moses, H G (1973) *Religion in Today's World*, Hart Davies
Palmer, M (1984) *Faiths and Festivals*, Ward Lock Educational
Parrinder, G (1974) *Worship in the World's Religions*, Sheldon Press
Smart, N (1974) *The Phenomenon of Religion*, MacMillan
Ward Lock Educational *Living Religions Series*

Buddhism	T Ling (1970)
Hinduism	Y Crompton (1971)
Islam	R El Droubie (1971)
Judaism	M Domnitz (1970)
Living Tribal Religions	H W Turner (1971)
The Orthodox Church	S Hackel (1971)
Protestant Christian Churches	M Ward (1970)
Roman Catholicism	P Kelly (1971)
Sikhism	W O Cole and P S Sambhi (1973)
Zen and Modern Japanese Religions	M Pye (1973)

Wolcott, L and C (1967) *Religions Around the World*, G Chapman Ltd

Religious Education 5–12

Useful Background Books for Teachers on the Bible

Alexander, D S and P J (Eds) (1983) *The Lion Handbook to the Bible*, Lion Publishing
Barclay, W and Zeffirelli, F (1977) *Jesus of Nazareth*, Collins
Bouquet, A C (Carousel Edition 1984) *Everyday Life in New Testament Times*, Carousel
Dale, A T (1978) *Portrait of Jesus*, Oxford University Press
Duncan, A (1974) *The Noble Heritage (Jerusalem)*, Longmans
Harker, R (1972) *Digging up the Bible Lands*, Bodley Head
Harrison, R K (1963) *Archaeology of the Old Testament*, Hodder and Stoughton
Magnusson, M *The Archaeology of the Bible*, BBC
de Vaux, R (1972) *The Bible and the Ancient Near East* Darton, Longman and Todd
Walton, R (Ed) (1970) *A Source Book of the Bible for Teachers*, SCM
Wilson, E (1955) *The Scrolls from the Dead Sea*, Collins
Yadin, Y (1966) *Masada*, Weidenfeld and Nicholson

Useful Books on Religious Education

Bradford Metropolitan District Council (1983)
Religious Education for Living in Today's World: Agreed Syllabus for RE
Cambridgeshire County Council (1982)
A Framework for Religious Education in Cambridgeshire
City of Manchester Education Department (1980)
Guidelines for Religious Education
Cole, W O (Ed) (1978) *World Faiths in Education*, G Allen and Unwin
Cox, E (1983) *Problems and Possibilities for Religious Education*, Hodder and Stoughton
Goldman, R J (1964) *Religious Understanding from Childhood to Adolescence*, Routledge and Kegan Paul
Goldman, R J (1965) *Readiness for Religion*, Routledge and Kegan Paul
Gower, R (1984) *Religious Education in the Junior Years*, Lion
Grimmit, M (1978) *What Can I do in RE?*, Mayhew McCrimmon
HMSO (1985) *Education for All* (the Swann Report), HMSO
Hertfordshire County Council (1981) *Hertfordshire Agreed Syllabus*
Holm, J (1975) *Teaching Religion in School*, Oxford University Press
Hull, J (1982) *New Directions in Religious Education*, Falmer Press

Hull, J (1984) *Studies in Religion and Education*, Falmer Press
Jackson, R (Ed) (1982) *Approaching World Religions*, John Murray
Laxton, W (Ed) *Paths to Understanding: A Handbook to Religious Education in Hampshire Schools*, Globe Educational
Lord, E and Bailey, C (1973) *A Reader in Religious and Moral Education*, SCM Press
Madge, V (1965) *Children in Search of Meaning*, SCM Press
Mumford, C (1979) Young Children and RE, E Arnold
Royal County of Berkshire (1982) *Religious Heritage and Personal Quest: Guidelines for RE*.
Schools' Council Working Paper 36 (1971) *Religious Education in the Secondary School*, MacMillan Educational
Schools Council (1977) *Discovering an Approach*, MacMillan Educational
Smart, N (1968) *Secular Education and the Logic of Religion*, Faber
Smart, N and Horder, D (1975) *New Movements in Religious Education*, Temple Smith
Sutcliffe, J M (1984) *A Dictionary of Religious Education*, SCM Press

Some Useful Addresses for RE Resources

RE Resources and In-Service Training Centre (DES)
Westhill College
Selly Oak
Birmingham B29 6LL

RE (In-Service Training and Resources) Centre (DES)
Lancaster House
West London Institute of Higher Education
Borough Road
Isleworth
Middlesex
TW7 5DU

National Society's RE Development Centre
23 Kensington Square
London
W8 5HN

York RE Centre
College of Ripon and York St John
Lord Mayor's Walk
York YO3 7EX

Board of Deputies of British Jews (Bookshop)
Woburn House
Upper Woburn Place
London WC1H OEP

Centre for World Development Education
128 Buckingham Palace Road
London
SW1W 9SH

Christian Education Movement
2 Chester House
Pages Lane
London N10 1PR

Global Enterprises
57 The Green
Southall
Middlesex (Sikh)

R Golub & Co Ltd
27 Osborn Street
London E16 TD (Jewish)

Independent Publishing Company
38 Kennington Lane
London SE11 4LS
(Indian Books and pictures)

Oberois Wholesale
101 The Broadway
Southall
Middlesex (Hindu and Sikh)

Pictorial Charts Educational Trust
27 Kirchen Road
West Ealing
London W13 OUD

Regents Park Mosque (Bookshop)
46 Park Road
London NW8

Soma Books
Commonwealth Institute
Kensington High Street
London W8 6NQ

Resources

SPCK Bookshop and Mail Order Service
Holy Trinity Church
Marylebone Road
London NW1 4DU (Branches throughout UK)

Index

age and understanding 18–23, 35, 116–7
artefacts 175–9

Bible 19, 20, 52
  background 119–23, 145
  history in 132–3
  teaching through 115–18
  'truth' of 124–6
birth and death
  Christian 53–4
  Hindu 61, 62–3
  Jewish 73–4
  Muslim 67–8
  Sikh 78

Canterbury Tales, The (Chaucer) 90
Christianity 51–6
  and festivals 99–107, 108–114
  in schools 8–9, 83
  in society 12–13
Christmas 28–9, 99–100, 110–14, 145
Creation 124, 125–6

Damien, Father 168
Daniel, Book of 127, 129–30, 136–7
Dead Sea Scrolls 123, 154–8
  teaching about 161–3
Diary of Anne Frank, The 69
Discovering an Approach 11
Durham Report, *The Fourth R* 11

Easter 28, 101–6, 177–9
Education Act, Butler (1944) 7
ethics 29, 32, 33

festivals
  Christian 52, 99–107, 145
  Hindu 59–60
  Jewish 71–2
  Muslim 67
  Sikh 77
  teaching of (Christian) 108–14, 177–9
  teaching through 82–3, 145

Goldman, R. 5, 35, 36, 115, 143
  research 16–23
gospels 139–41
Granth Sahib 74–5, 77, 78
Grimmit, M. 23, 35, 36

Harrison, R. K. 132n
Hinduism 27, 56–63
Huddleston, Trevor 166, 168

I Am David (Anne Holm) 96
Islam 25, 27, 63–8

Jesus 51
  life of 139–41
  teaching about 145–8
Jonah, Book of 127–9
journeys 93–4

Index

Judaism 27, 29, 30, 32, 68–74
  as theme 84–5

Kolbe, Maximilian 167–8

legends 126–7, 135–6
Lourdes 31, 89

Madge, V. 17n
marriage
  Christian 54
  Hindu 62
  Jewish 73
  Muslim 68
  Sikh 78
Marx, Karl 24
Marxism 25–6
Masada 151–4
  teaching about 158–61
miracles 141–2, 147
monasticism 56
Moses and the Burning Bush 31, 32, 39
multicultural schools 12, 13–14, 80, 81–3, 166
Muslims
  see Islam
myths 28–9, 124–6
  teaching of 134–5

Nash, P. 116n
Ninny's Boat (Clive King) 95–6

Pandora 125
parables 119, 142–4
  teaching of 148–50
Peatling, J. H. 22
Piaget 18, 21, 22, 33
pilgrimages 30, 31, 88–98
  literature of 95–8
  Muslim 66–7
  see also Lourdes; Walsingham
Pilgrim's Progress, The (John Bunyan) 88, 97–8
Priestly, J. G. 116n
prophets 130–1

  teaching about 137
psalms 133–4

Ramadan 10, 80–1
Readiness for Religion (R. Goldman) 17, 19
religion
  definition of 24–6, 38
    as six-dimensional 26–32, 164
    for teaching 32–4
  as living activity 164–5
  teaching 165–9
  understanding 3, 10–11
Religious Thinking from Childhood to Adolescence (R. Goldman) 17
Ruth, Book of 127, 128

Samson 126–7
school
  and church 7, 13
  syllabus 7–8, 12–13, 115
Sikhism 74–8, 82
Silver Sword, The (Ian Seraillier) 97
Smart, Ninian 27
Swann Report, *Education for All* 1

teaching
  aims 6–7, 9, 11, 13–15, 32–3
  approaches 6–7, 9–11, 81–7
  books for 179–80
  about Jesus 139, 145–50
  resources 170–9
    addresses for 191–2
  see also themes; Bible; festivals; myths; parables; pilgrimages, etc.
Ten Commandments 69–70, 164
themes
  examples of 39–47, 84–7, 120, 121–3
  life and depth 35–7
  place in RE 37–40
  see also Bible; festivals; pilgrimages

Walsingham (Norfolk) 90–3

195

Index

Wesley, John 31
Wilson, E. 83n
worship 29–30
   Christian 53

Hindu 58–9
Muslim 65–6
places of 170–1
visiting 171–4

For Product Safety Concerns and Information please contact our EU
representative GPSR@taylorandfrancis.com
Taylor & Francis Verlag GmbH, Kaufingerstraße 24, 80331 München, Germany

www.ingramcontent.com/pod-product-compliance
Lightning Source LLC
Chambersburg PA
CBHW051644230426
43669CB00013B/2431